Echoes
from My Prairie

*E*choes
from My Prairie

Ardeth G. Kapp

Bookcraft
Salt Lake City, Utah

Library of Congress Catalog Card Number:
79-53128
ISBN 0-88494-384-4

Lithographed in the United States of America
PUBLISHERS PRESS
Salt Lake City, Utah

To those wonderful people, with their rich insights of life and their generous sharing, in the beautiful little village on the Western Canadian prairie—Glenwood

Contents

Preface

Lead me,
Guide me,
Walk beside me,
Help me find the way. . . .

This expression from the LDS song by Naomi Randall, "I Am a Child of God," is the constant plea of child or adult yearning to be taught—reaching for knowledge, hungering for reassurance, striving toward perfection with the hope of receiving gentle encouragement along the way.

Who will teach them? How will they find their way? That primary responsibility is placed by divine decree with parents.

I have commanded you to bring up your children in light and truth. (D&C 93:40.)

In the press of this last quarter of the twentieth century, that responsibility seems at times almost overwhelming. Yet I believe that life in any century presents a myriad of experiences which may either be passed over unconsciously or savored as the very substance through which the profound purposes of life are transmitted and realized. The wonders of creation, the symbolism of the Resurrection, and the witness of the recurring seasons are not reserved only for those growing up on an eighty-acre farm—they are inherent in the smallest window box. But it is a sensitive teacher, preferably a parent, who helps in the discovery.

Lessons in economics at the candy counter, endless waiting for the birthday that allows for the first date or use of the family car, the adventures in and secrets of the rooms in Grandmother's house—such common experiences shared in the family relationship become the setting for the most profound learning in a child's life. The common incidents, added one after the other, echo and re-echo as the child grows; and those experiences become the reservoir from which lasting attitudes and values are drawn.

My hope in sharing these cherished family experiences with you is that you will discover your own echoes from the past and increase your sensitivity to the daily experiences which will supply the echoes for your future.

With that sensitivity it is possible to fill the yearning—

Teach me all that I must do,
To live with Him someday.

Acknowledgments

Deep appreciation is expressed to my friend Judith Smith not only for reacting to and refining the manuscript but also for providing me with encouragement and helpful suggestions; and to my friend Kathleen Pulsipher for her skill in capturing the mood of the written word through her sensitive illustrations.

Sticks and Stones

During the summer months when it seemed that the sun never went to bed, and after the chores were done and the cows returned to the pastures, as if by appointment the kids of all ages gathered in the open field not far from our house. With the approach of evening the whole atmosphere appeared to change along with our activity. Even the sounds and smells seemed to be in harmony with this magical hour. The odor of burning leaves or of sweet clover mingled with alfalfa, hardly noticeable during the day, became an important part of the evening setting.

The rhythmic sounds of childhood filled the air as each one found himself chanting the phrases that announced his particular play. The heavy rope hummed a constant beat against the hardened earth while young voices called out in unison, "Mabel, Mabel, set the table; don't forget the salt and pepper," at which time the beat was quickened for a minute. Then, with precision efficiency the rope turners reverted to the original beat and someone else took a turn.

An old granary, located in the corner of the open field, became a valuable part of our prairie playground. It was just the right size to present a real challenge as we strained every muscle to throw the ball clear over the top—and if we didn't make it, the slope of the roof brought the ball right back, and we'd call out to our friends on the other side, "Antie, come back!"

The delay between the announcement that we had thrown the ball as we'd called, "Antie," and then the waiting before announcing whether we were successful in getting it over made an interesting break in the rhythm carried on the evening air. The very inflection in the voice clearly identified success or failure in that attempt as we heard, "Antie I over," or "Antie come back." The moment the ball went out of sight over the top to the downward slope of the other side, the air was still; and our hearts began to beat faster as we wondered if someone on the other side had caught the ball. We tried to look at both corners of the granary at once and to prepare to run safely around to the other side without getting caught. That anxious moment was broken and normal breathing resumed only when the chant from the other side could be heard, "Antie I over, antie come back."

Even the birds, especially the meadowlarks perched on the barbed-wire fence or the telephone lines, added variation to the chorus of contrasting sounds and rhythms of the evening. I had been taught, and a good ear could verify, that the meadowlarks unmistakably announced in sweet cadence: "This is a pretty little town. This is a pretty little town." And certainly with their view of our buildings and open fields, the pronouncement had to be true.

From the front porches of our homes, our parents need only listen for a moment to be informed of our current activity. Only an extended silence might warrant further investigation. From those same porches the calls were made which were so much resisted and which always came at the worst time: "Come in now. It's time to come in."

That was my signal. About the same time each evening and without variation in the words or tone, like picking up the lines in a play, I responded, always in the same pleading tone,

"Oh, Mom, not yet!" And she continued the familiar dialogue, "Okay, just ten more minutes." It seemed to me that my mom always started the series that brought calls from the other porches until most of the younger kids were in. I often wondered just how long we could have stayed out if my mom hadn't started it all.

Inside, from my bedroom window, I could see our open field still bathed in the full light of that Canadian summer sun which seemed to be teasing me by continuing its warm rays long after my painful curfew. The window opened wide enough to let in fresh air, but with it came the joyful sounds of the older kids which served now to tantalize me in my sorrowful plight.

I watched as the bigger kids gathered in a circle with their fists outstretched. I knew they were choosing up sides as one of them began to chant, "One potato, two potato, three potato, four, five potato, six potato, seven potato more." The last person hit on "seven potato more" was eliminated from the group. This procedure continued until only one person remained, and by then the next game was in progress. Hide and seek was a favorite—I always wondered how anyone could count from one to ten so fast before shouting, "All eyes open, here I come." Frequently the last game of the evening, as I remember, was run, sheep, run. My brother and the other older kids played it for hours and hours. It seemed to me they never had to come in.

We didn't always play in the open field, although that became our official meeting place. There were many areas that called us from all directions. After supper one evening during the latter part of the summer, just before harvest time, I stood with a friend on top of the big dirt mound that covered our root cellar located just next to the clothesline. Together we taunted several other girls as we pushed them down the side of the root cellar. Kobie, my neighbor, and her cousins attempted to climb up one side as we shouted: "We're the boss of Bunker's Hill. We can fight and we can kill!" This challenging declaration,

repeated in mocking tones, became a source of irritation to those below, and with increased determination they tried to get to the top and push us off. When our position looked threatened, I immediately announced that it was our root cellar anyway, and they couldn't play on it anymore! This only intensified the struggle.

The friendly chants of our other childhood activities were not part of this experience. Words were called that gave expression to troubled and mounting feelings. Kobie and her friends said we were cheating, and she called us names. I immediately reminded her that her mother was from Holland and talked funny. Someone picked up a rotten potato from the pile that had been cleared out of the root cellar and threw it, and then another potato was thrown, and another, and another.

By now the destructive chants were being repeated first by one side and then the other, such as "Sticks and stones can break my bones, but names can never hurt me." By this time my friend and I were emerging as the winners, and Kobie and her friends were shouting through their tears. As we all left the root cellar and went our separate ways, it was an awful feeling even to be a winner.

The next day when I had to explain to Dad why the potatoes were scattered all over the ground, he seemed to understand much more than I reported to him. He asked a lot of questions that were hard to answer. In my mind it was all Kobie's fault. Now I was in trouble, and I was determined to get even with her. My friends and I had decided we didn't need Kobie and her friends, and that was that. And then we began looking for things to justify our decision. She dressed differently. And besides, her mom talked funny. Her dad was a shoemaker who tanned smelly leather hides, while my dad was a farmer who raised turkeys.

The following evening Dad took me by the hand and we headed toward the turkey pens. I had gone with him many times before, but his silence on this occasion caused me to feel uneasy as I tried to anticipate the unknown.

We stood quietly by the fence, and I waited. Finally, Dad spoke. "See those turkeys over there in the corner?" he asked, pointing to a small bunch against the fence. I nodded. "I want you to watch them for a few minutes."

We stood in silence as I watched what I had seen a few times before. One turkey was pecking on the back of the head of another one. After repeated peckings, blood came to the surface on the afflicted bird. This drew the attention of the other turkeys, who now joined in until all were pecking on the same turkey on the same wounded spot. I stared at the turkeys in silence until I felt quite uncomfortable. Then Dad broke the silence.

"Do you know why those turkeys are all pecking on that one poor turkey?" he asked. And without waiting for an answer, he continued: "It usually means they are in need of something. There may be something lacking in their diet. When that's the case, the first step is to try to give them what they need so they'll stop this terrible thing. I also have to put a tarlike salve on the wound of the injured turkey so the wound can be protected until it heals."

Dad went on, "If the other turkeys continue to peck on this bird or other birds, there is something else we can do." I listened, curious. "We can take the wounded bird out and move it away from the others so it will have a chance to heal. But the real concern is for the birds that are doing the pecking, because if they're not stopped they could destroy a whole flock of valuable turkeys. If they can't be trained, they have to be controlled." He paused. "There is a last resort."

All of a sudden, I remembered the last resort. I knew what had to happen to those birds. I had seen it done often, but hadn't understood why. Months before, I had watched Dad take something that looked like electric clippers from a shelf in the turkey coop, while my brother would catch one of the turkeys that had been pecking on the others. He would hold it securely under his arm while Dad seared off the sharp tip of its beak. Then my brother would release it back into the flock,

6

now harmless because it could not peck anymore. I remembered the awful smell; I had always wondered why those dumb birds would do such a stupid thing. They deserved to have their beak tips burned off, I thought.

Dad shifted his position. He was no longer looking at the turkeys; he was looking straight at me.

"Sometimes people, and not just children," he explained, "will begin to say unkind things about someone. They begin to peck on them and then others join in the pecking, and before long a sore can develop. Not one that you can see on the outside, but one that causes a lot of hurting inside. Not only does it hurt the person who is suffering such unkindness but, even more, it can destroy the person who allows those kinds of thoughts and words to get in his head. Do you know what I mean?" he asked.

Immediately I remembered the awful feeling inside when I threw the potatoes and told Kobie and her friends to get off our root cellar and go home. Although Dad had not mentioned Kobie and the incident of that dreadful day, there was no doubt in my mind that had it not happened all this concern for the turkeys would never have come up.

It wasn't long after this incident that we heard that Kobie and her family were going to move to another town. A few days later I stood by the white picket fence that separated our yards and watched her dad and brothers load the truck that would carry all their belongings away. Kobie would go too, I thought, and her mom and dad. It was okay, now, that her mom spoke differently; and I remembered that she did have a beautiful singing voice; and I loved the way her dad could put soles on old shoes that would make them look new. I didn't want Kobie to go.

I wondered deep inside if I were responsible for this move, and thought of the turkeys that had to be moved to another location so their wounds could heal. And I also thought of what happened to the turkeys who didn't stop pecking the other birds.

7

I wanted to cry, and I wanted Kobie to stay. I wanted her to climb on our root cellar again. I wanted her to slide down our cellar door. I wanted to turn the rope for her while she jumped. But that evening Kobie and her family left their home. They left our neighborhood and our town. A lot of people gathered around to say good-bye, and everyone seemed happy. But I didn't say good-bye. I just watched and watched. And when Kobie looked my way, I raised my hand just a little and waved. Kobie waved back, and somehow I hoped she knew I was sorry—very, very sorry.

Do You Hear What I Hear?

I sat straight up in my bed, my heart pounding, my eyes as big as saucers, staring into the darkness of my bedroom in the middle of the night. The fact that this incident had occurred several times over the past few weeks only added to the fright that left me paralyzed for the moment.

This was not "just my imagination" (the explanation that had been given to my insistence that I heard strange sounds in the middle of the night). Tomorrow I would find the answer to this mystery. I could no longer try to believe that, just because no one else could hear it, I really didn't hear what I thought I heard. I was not dreaming. I was wide awake, and my senses could not deny my experience.

The next morning Dad held me securely by the ankles while lowering me carefully into the dark cistern. Except for my little sisters, I was the only one who could fit through the small opening at the top. Anyway, it was I who had insisted on this investigation. I knew there was something or someone alive in this dark hole filled with water.

Our cistern had been constructed with the addition on our house. It was a waterproof concrete room, like a basement, located under what became my bedroom.

With a flashlight held tightly in one hand and bracing myself against the damp wall inside the cistern with the other, I began my daring search. *What if I did find something?* I thought. My anxiety increased even more as I considered the alternative. *What if I didn't?* It's uncomfortable and even scary sometimes to stand alone when no one else hears what you hear or knows what you know. Even though no one else had ever heard it, still at infrequent intervals I heard splashing sounds in the cistern under my bedroom. I had summoned various members of the family on different occasions to come and listen. Each time they listened, they heard nothing. But at those times neither did I. On one occasion, when I had asked Grandma to listen just once more in hopes of having a witness to this mystery, she said she thought maybe she could hear something. But then Grandma was hard of hearing, and at that time there were no sounds in the cistern that I could detect.

The water supply in our town was hauled from the river in large barrels during the winter. In the summer we could use all the water we wanted from the ditches that bordered the margin of our field. Our whole town was measured off by ditches running north and south, east and west. From these ditches we obtained our water supply.

In the late fall it was very important to make sure the cistern was filled to capacity before the precious water quit running. The ditch along the north end of the field behind our house provided our major source of water. A barbed-wire fence running parallel to the ditch kept the cows away from the water supply. In the early spring of the year a prolific crop of yellow dandelions would creep under the fence and mingle gracefully with the tall grass along the ditch banks.

A large metal pipe with a very fine screen over the end provided the conduit from the ditch to our cistern. Over the other end of the pipe inside the cistern a very fine mesh material was securely tied to prevent any foreign matter from getting into our water supply.

"I just don't see how anything could possibly get by that

screen," Dad explained. And like an echo my brother chided, "Nothing could get by that screen."

Their reasoning did not change my assurance of what I had heard. The fact that they had not heard the noise made it very difficult to explain—but it did not stop the splashing nor my ears from hearing it. I didn't know what I would do if I found no explanation to the mystery of the cistern, but before I faced that possibility I had to make a thorough investigation.

As I was hanging upside down, my brother made teasing inquiries. "Is there a dragon in there, or maybe a sea monster?"

With my ankles hurting now from Dad's firm grip and my eyes feeling enlarged from being upside down, I feared I might have to abandon my mission before completion. Just then the beam from the flashlight exposed the water level against the outside wall of the cistern along the north side. At that moment I heard a familiar splash, a big one, and then another and another. Dad heard it also. Even my brother admitted hearing it. My once-foolish investigation now drew greater interest.

From outside the question was repeated over and over: "What is it? What is it?"

There it was, right before my eyes. I had been the only one to hear it, and now I was the only one who could see it. In the corner at the water's edge, held captive in the beam of the flashlight and splashing furiously, was a dark and frightened muskrat.

The mystery had been solved as far as I was concerned. Dad lifted me carefully out of the cistern, and I told in detail what I had seen during my investigation. Dad remained very puzzled about how a muskrat could have possibly ended up in our water supply, but the fact that it had was enough to quiet my concerns.

Retrieving the foreigner from the cistern became the immediate task at hand. The next problem was what to do with the muskrat. Of course, by now my brother had designs on it. Dad made a quick determination. Since I was the only one who had heard it and since I had held firm to my conviction even when nobody else could hear it, the muskrat would be mine. I could do with it as I wished.

Years later, having moved away from my prairie home, I returned in the spring of the year for an important event. My dear aunt had become ill and passed away. It was a cold day. The remaining winter snow was dirty, and the bare ground appeared desolate.

As I stood quietly by her grave in the cemetery, I thought again of childhood days spent in the garden under the tree. My feelings told me that childhood was only yesterday, yet my reasoning assured me that many years had passed ever so quickly. I pondered the passing of time, then looked around to see others quietly meditating, each considering his own thoughts, perhaps reflecting, searching, or even seeking. Their thoughts were unknown to me, as mine were to them. In the chilly wind, people clutched their coats around their necks and kept their backs to the wind. For a time I withdrew into my own thoughts.

12

In the quiet of that peaceful setting I heard in my mind sounds as real as the splashing of a muskrat. Faintly at first, but as I waited and strained to listen, just like the sounds from the cistern under my bedroom they came again and then again. Like words in my mind, I heard clearly: "Life passes ever so quickly, and there is no time to waste. You would do well to prepare for the future. Go back to college and complete your education, and do it now." While this thought had crossed my mind before, it was not until that moment that the impression, like a loud splash, would no longer be quieted.

After returning home to the routine of familiar schedules, I soon realized that the challenge was not so much to accept what I knew and had heard, but to attempt to give a reasonable explanation to family, friends and co-workers; and then, after hearing their many questions, to guard against losing direction as I repeated those same questions to myself.

"But why would you give up an excellent position with a big company to start back to school, almost from the beginning?"

"Do you realize many college graduates would be anxious for the management position you now have? What will you gain from college that you don't already have?"

"What about your seniority?"

"Are you sure this is a wise choice? Why don't you think about it for a while, maybe wait until fall and see if you still feel the same."

My impressions were foreign to anyone else, but why shouldn't they be? No one else heard the muskrat under my bedroom either. Yet I'm sure they would have if it had been under their bedroom. The fact that I could not explain what I heard did not stop the splashing. And so it was now with my urgent feeling to respond and follow through with my promptings even though the explanations might sound unreasonable. Maybe someday this seeming mystery would also be solved. Then I could better understand it myself and explain it to those who were now asking the questions. Until then, I would keep listening and following.

Over the next three years, during times of struggle and distraction that made the goal seem almost too far off, even unreasonable and hardly worth the effort, I would listen for the signal that would keep me going.

It is long after the personal and private victory that rewards for one's efforts become public. As I neared graduation, the recognition and praise no longer needed were freely given by many. Like a light shining in a darkened cistern revealing the explanation for the continuous splashing, the impressions that had given direction to my efforts began coming together like pieces of a mosaic. Preparation and opportunities never before dreamed of converged at the crossroads at a moment in time that gave meaning and purpose to all the previous splashing that would not be quieted.

I knew of no explanation for what might be in the future for me. But, then, not until after I had looked into the cistern could I explain the muskrat either.

"Wherefore, dispute not because ye see not," wrote Moroni, "for ye receive no witness until after the trial of your faith." (Ether 12:6.)

Fences

From the top of our hill we could see for miles and miles in every direction. Like a great patchwork quilt, fields stretched out in a variety of colors extending into the far distant horizon. It was a clear day, and I traced the thin line of the horizon around full circle until I came back to where I had started— back to our project of fence building.

"Fences make good neighbors, you know," was Dad's comment as he continued tamping the black rich soil firmly with the end of the shovel handle around a cedar post that I had just helped him set in place. We had been working since early morning, but there was still a pile of cedar posts to be placed in holes yet to be dug. It looked to me as if ten or twelve posts would be needed to finish the fence along the south end of our alfalfa patch.

Before locating the spot for the next hole, Dad took a few steps backward and then leaned forward, squinting one eye while sighting along the fence line as he double-checked with the accuracy of a plumb line the quality of our work. Determined to locate the position for the next hole (before Dad again repeated his familiar instructions), I quickly took my bearings by looking in the opposite direction from him. In my mind I rehearsed the steps that I had heard over and over again. "You begin from where you are—that's the last post you set. Now, if you look just to the distance of the next hole, your distance might be right but your direction could be all wrong." And then he would explain, "It's the direction that's even more important than the distance between the posts if you want to have a straight fence." And patiently he would repeat: "See that point out on the horizon that never moves? Keep your eye on that. Rest your eyes on a fixed target and line up the posts with that marker. Then you'll build a straight fence."

Following his instructions from memory, I marched out through the alfalfa to what I thought was the proper distance and the right direction. Confidently I planted one foot ahead of the other, marked the exact location, and waited for Dad's response. With few words this time and a smile on his face, he simply confirmed my accuracy by placing the shovel at the very tip of my boot and began digging.

With a rightful sense of success and increased confidence, I became more interested in the project of fence building.

"Dad," I asked, "if the direction is right and the distance is right and the posts are securely in place, does that make a good fence?"

"It all depends," he said.

"Depends on what?" I questioned.

"It depends on the purpose for the fence—and how it's to be used," he answered.

As always, Dad was not just performing a task; he was providing an experience—and how much any of his children learned was not necessarily related to the size of the job to be done.

By midmorning I was anxiously anticipating our rest break, when Dad announced that it was time for a drink I quickly brought the old burlap-wrapped jug of water from the cab of the truck. The covering that we soaked in the irrigation ditch to help keep the contents of the jug cool was now almost dry, but that wonderful smell of the damp burlap was still there as Dad held the jug to my mouth while the cool water poured out. "Good stuff," he said after he had taken his turn and replaced the cap on what we called our special treat.

Together we sat at the brow of the hill. He always picked a blade of grass and then began chewing on the end as if it were a part of the rest-break ceremony. I did the same. After a few minutes of quiet surveillance, Dad began thinking aloud: "We'll have a good fence around our eighty acres when we're finished, Ardie, but that needn't keep us bound in. Our possessions go far beyond this." I didn't know for sure what he meant, but I knew he would continue to share his thoughts. That was the reward, along with the drink and the lunch under the elm trees, that made a day at the farm with Dad a happy and memorable experience.

Stretching his arm to full length, his forefinger extended, he began at the far left and made a sweeping motion that covered the broad expanse in front of us. "This is our real domain," he explained. "This clear, blue sky miles and miles above our heads is ours to enjoy. See those rugged Canadian Rockies with their snowcapped peaks?" he said, pointing to the far southwest, "they're a rightful part of our territory also. And the birds," he continued, "those that build their nests in our elm trees or just traverse our meadow and pasture. They, too, are a part of our abundant wealth." And then, as if to secure my understanding of our vast inventory, he reminded me also of our sunsets that cast a glow across the huge prairie sky and explained that no obstruction or fence can limit our real domain. "Unless," he added, "we ourselves put up boundaries and fences that close our rich resources out."

My questioning expression brought a further explanation. "Inside fences, Ardie, invisible to others, are very real. They can sometimes hold us captive," he cautioned. "And furthermore, they are impossible to take down unless we ourselves determine to do it." Then, looking out again at our extended wealth, he seemed to be pondering as he added one more comment before changing the subject. "It's sometimes a hard job to take down a fence. It may take a lifetime."

As late afternoon approached, Dad pulled his watch from the little pocket in his overalls. "It's time to call it quits," he announced; and be began putting the tools in the back of the old blue truck. Sitting side by side, we bounced along over the ruts that had been left in the dirt road following the last rain storm. A cloud of dust trailed behind us as we headed down the three-mile stretch to our home.

"You're a good helper," he said; and I knew he really meant it. "We do good work together," he continued, "and today we learned a lot about fences." I wasn't sure what he meant. Now weary of fence building, I decided to leave the responsibility for that lesson to Dad. If it was important, I knew he would bring it up again.

It was nearing the end of the school year, almost a full season since our experience of fence building. For me it had been a long, hard winter—a season of harsh temperatures and many storms. It's true that the thermometer did not record such adversities, but I knew that the severity of any Canadian blizzard could never be more threatening to a human being than the devastation I had repeatedly experienced at school that year. I remember the occasion, following a weekly examination, when every student's name was written on the chalkboard in the hall for everyone to see. The names did not appear in alphabetical order, but in rank order—the highest at the top, the lowest in the most conspicuous place of all, the bottom. Even with my name in that horrifying spot, I felt a faint twinge of gratitude for the only two names that followed mine on the list (in spite of the fact that these two were German students who were struggling with the language).

One day after school as I stood at our kitchen window looking out on a world that seemed so destructive and cruel, I could hear my mother reaching for words that might help quiet the storm she knew was raging inside me. "But you must realize," she said, "that you've missed so much school. You've been ill and . . . and . . ." All her explanations made little difference to me when in my hand I had the evidence (my report card) to confirm my conviction that I was dumb and that the whole world, at least all my friends, knew it.

Dad called me into the living room, and I sat on the footstool in front of his big chair. Leaning forward, he spoke in an almost pleading tone. "I have a concern," he confessed.

"What is it, Dad?" I asked, fearing that his concern was for my report card.

Taking both my hands in his big hands and looking at me as if to see clear through me, without any explanation or elaboration, he simply said, "Before the last day of school, I want you to go to Mrs. Shane and express appreciation for all she has tried to teach you this year."

"But, Dad," I exploded, "don't you understand?"

He nodded and said, "I do."

And then like steam escaping from a valve under pressure, I began: "But Mrs. Shane hates me. She failed me. She hasn't been fair. She always asks me why I can't be like my brother. Dad, I can't." In a final cry of anguish I sobbed, "I hate her!"

Dad again just nodded, and with more feeling this time said, "I know you do."

We sat in silence for a long time. I struggled with the unbelievable request from my father who I thought loved me, while he searched our shared reservoir of experiences for just the right mortar to make his reasoning hold together. With a faraway look in his eye and with his ability to recreate in vivid detail our most treasured experiences together, he began, "Remember the time last fall when we were fence builders together?" That reminder was a partial relief to my troubled heart. I nodded. "And do you remember that we talked about inside fences and how hard it is to take them down?" That was the part I couldn't remember. I guess he thought that in this setting it had some application and he tried again.

He told me about how he understood my feelings and how he had watched me struggle with school and with my teacher, Mrs. Shane. "Now about the fence, Ardie," he explained,

19

getting right to the point. "As you have struggled with your lessons and made considerable progress, I have been very proud of you; but I have also watched you gradually build a fence, one post at a time. A fence that should never have been built at all. It will limit you. It will keep you confined and hold you in and restrict your progress. It is an inside fence, Ardie, and only you can take it down and only if you want to."

How could he know all this? I had never complained at home about my teacher. I knew better than that. How did he know how I felt inside? His seriousness prompted me to ask the question he had hoped for. "But how can I do it, Dad?"

And then he went back to where he had started as he repeated: "Before the last day of school I want you to go to Mrs. Shane and express appreciation for all she has tried to teach you this year. You don't have to do it today or even tomorrow. There are ten days before the end of school, and a fence isn't put up or taken down in a day."

The remaining ten days were silently numbered without any prodding from Dad. One evening as a family everyone talked about hard things they had each done, fences they had taken down. Dad told us about a problem he had through a misunderstanding with a neighbor, and I learned for the first time why he secretly shoveled our neighbor's walk each morning after a snow storm before anyone else was up. I always thought he was just clearing the walk, but he explained that he was taking down a fence.

The next morning in our family prayer, my mom asked for special help for each of us. At that moment I thought I might be able to take down a fence, maybe even that day. I would see.

I sat all day in school as Mrs. Shane in her usual way tried to get the attention of the students by embarrassing them and shouting at them. "Priscilla," she said, "your voice is so loud you could stand on your porch and call all over town without a telephone." In the afternoon it was Harvey who was the victim of her wrath. "Harvey," she shouted from her desk in the center of the room, "if all your brains were put in a bullet there wouldn't be enough powder to blow your hat off." No, I couldn't take the fence down today, I thought, maybe tomorrow.

Somehow thinking about fences and the good day Dad and I had spent together building ours last fall eased the feelings inside for a moment at least. Dad was right. It's the inside fences we build ourselves that bind us. Maybe Mrs. Shane had lots of inside fences that kept her troubled and cross, I thought. I surely didn't want to be like that.

Finally the school bell rang. All the kids left immediately. They always did. No one stays to talk to a teacher they don't like. I fussed around my desk to purposely delay until, except for Mrs. Shane and me, the room was empty. Looking up from her desk and glancing over her glasses she said with a crisp voice, "Well?"

Without really seeing her (only anticipating my joy when I would see Mom and Dad after school that night), I hurried up the aisle to her desk. Standing with my head down, not looking at this teacher I had learned to fear and even hate, I blurted out my message that would, I hoped, take down the fence and no more. "Mrs. Shane," I said, my heart pounding against my chest, "I want to tell you thanks for trying to teach me, even if I didn't learn." With my message delivered I was free to run from that threatening position and, as I hoped, never have to talk to her again.

But before I could escape, she reached for my hand and drew me to her. She put her arm around my waist, but I felt myself pulling back. She waited a minute which seemed like an hour. "Thank you," she said in a quiet voice that didn't sound like my teacher's voice at all.

I glanced up to see her face. *Can this be Mrs. Shane?* I thought. She looked different, not so scary, more sad. Her eyes looked unhappy. She even sounded different. We visited a minute before I left. *Just three days before the end of school,* I thought, and now I wondered why I had never really seen her before.

I ran all the way home from the school, down the path, across the stile, through the open field by the church, past the gooseberry bushes in front of the Bucks' home, and past the Woods' white horse. Without slackening my pace, I licked two fingers on my right hand, stamped the palm of my left hand, and hit my left hand with my fist for good luck. I rounded the corner by the garage into our backyard where Dad was fixing a picket fence for the sweet peas to climb. Quite out of breath, I wondered how I would report my victory.

Dad had adjusted from his kneeling position to sit on the ground and with his arms outstretched and a big smile on his face he said: "Well, tell me about it, 'fence wrecker.' How was it?" We sat on the ground together while I caught my breath. He listened to all of the details, interrupting only to ask me occasionally just how I felt at a particular time; and then he would nod and continue to look at me over his heavy eyebrows.

Having heard the full report carefully recited, Dad, searching my eyes, questioned me, "And how do you feel about Mrs. Shane, my dear?"

"I don't hate her, Dad," I honestly confessed.

He smiled and nodded, "The rest will come."

The Secrets Within

Like sentinels in the distance, our rugged mountain peaks could be seen always in place against the southwestern sky. Every morning they were there on duty, spanning our frontiers of many miles and providing a welcome break in the vast expanse that otherwise might have let our prairie go on forever.

Old Chief Mountain stood in a position of prominence, seeming to dwarf the other mountains that stretched out on either side. That mountain often took on the dual aspect of a royal monarch pondering all of his subjects from far and near, while serving simultaneously as a marker for our little village by giving location and position in relation to the vast prairie extending from us in all directions.

There were days during the late fall when the mountains, wrapped in a brooding mist, revealing only their peaks like a darkened silhouette against the distant sky, appeared to be dressing for a special occasion. On clear days another side of their ever-changing mood was exposed. Their snowcapped peaks then provided a sharp contrast to their deep blue formations that could be seen clearly even at a distance. These mountains appeared timeless, filled with the secrets of those who had come and gone before. During the summer they drew us like magnets.

Around our campfires, as the firelight played against his face, Dad would often acquaint us with some of the Indian lore of the area. But even more interesting were the stories he told of his own experiences, the challenges of winter that "tested the endurance of man and beast to the very limit." Sitting on the stump of a log, he would hold us breathless as his tales of truth and courage unfolded.

"The winter of 1922," he began one evening, "was a tough one. We were making a trip to the Victory Mines for coal, about forty miles distance. It was cold enough to curl the ears of a timber wolf."

Sometimes, if the sound effects were timed just right, the howl of a distant coyote could draw the color from our faces, observable even by firelight. When that happened, Dad would always wait a minute to allow full impact of the added effect before going on.

"That evening," he continued, "it was forty-seven degrees below zero when we finally arrived at the mine." He rubbed his hands together by the fire as if he were still feeling the savage effect of that bitter cold. "We gratefully accepted the hospitality of the people who lived there. Inside their little cabin we could still hear the howling wind that threatened our lives." He shifted his position a little to break the serious mood and continued with a smile. "There was an older fellow there who put his bedroll near mine. As tired as I was, I woke up twice during the night thinking the house was falling in. His snoring was like thunder in a Rocky Mountain canyon."

We always identified our favorite stories by the year they occurred. "Dad," I requested, "tell us about the year 1919."

It was as if he were relating it for the first time, and we listened with the same intense interest as he began: "Winter closed in early that year and people from all of the southern Alberta area needed feed for their animals. There was just not

24

enough to go around. Feed got so short that I couldn't keep my team well. They started to get thin and weak. I couldn't stand to push them half-fed through the tough roads in that bitter cold, so I gave my contract for driving the children to school to the Hartleys. During that winter one of their horses died on the road in the deep snow while lugging the children home from school." His voice always softened when he told that part of the story.

Dad's reservoir of experiences seemed limitless, and around the campfire he shared examples of courage and determination that seemed to establish a level of expectation for all who were born to live in those parts. Usually, as the embers would die down, he would reach into his store of poetry and recite a few of his favorite lines from Robert Service's poem "The Law of the Yukon."

> "Send not your foolish and feeble; send me your
>   strong and your sane—
> Send me the best of your breeding, lend me
>   your chosen ones;
> Them will I take to my bosom, them will I
>   call my sons;"

I didn't recall the next part until he came to the lines that I thought I could fully understand from my own experience:

> "Staggering blind through the storm-whirl,
>   stumbling mad through the snow,"

And then came the lines that sounded to me as if they had been written about my own dad.

> "And I wait for the men who will win me—and I
>   will not be won in a day;
> And I will not be won by weaklings, subtle,
>   suave and mild,
> But by men with the hearts of vikings, and the
>   simple faith of a child."

His dramatic interpretation made his words burn into my heart like fire and somehow awakened a sense of courage within. I thought of the times I had frozen my cheeks and my eyelashes while walking to school through the blinding snow with the temperature at forty below; and then after school being forced homeward by the north wind from the back, while the mountains in the distance, covered with snow and ice, stood like giant sepulchers for the less courageous. I felt that I knew something of the test of endurance and vowed that I would not be found wanting when the roll call for courage was taken.

During the month of August, when I was fourteen years old, Dad and I decided to carry out our dreams to explore these mountains and become acquainted with the intimate secrets they kept from those who chose to remain at a distance. Our plans expanded to include four of my girl friends, LaNore, Judy, Maida, and Orva, who had or could get saddle horses. Orva's mother and dad came too. Altogether there were eight in our party. Along with our saddle horses, we took one faithful packhorse that carried the supplies which would sustain us for the eight-day trip. We covered the pack with a big canvas and anchored it securely with ropes carefully tied together with a diamond hitch knot. We all mastered the art of tying the diamond hitch. It was only the first of a multitude of new experiences we would have before our return.

We were driven to the mouth of Yarrow Canyon in trucks and then, anticipating the unknown, we headed up the trail in single file, one horse following the other. We talked with some concern about riding a horse most of the day for eight consecutive days.

Once into the mountains we began to see and feel and experience things we had not even anticipated. It was as if scales were falling from our eyes as the colors, shapes, sounds, and smells crowded in to be part of this great adventure. The silver drops of dew left on the freshly washed leaves in the morning, the bubbling song of the crowned kinglet of midday, the shadows of the evening advancing along the rocks, and the whispering pines at night all added to this vision that was opening up before us.

On the evening of the third glorious day we found ourselves in what we reverently named our "pine tree cathedral." Not until then would I have fully recognized its beauty, I think. I needed time for letting go of the familiar experiences that crowded the mind with familiar thoughts; a time for opening up to receive the unfamiliar; and then a preparation of heart and soul to reach out for all that was to be offered. Here, tucked away from the world, we had discovered this small clearing in the heart of a pine forest. Tall, stately trees towered heavenward, casting shadows in stained-glass-window effects on the spongy ground carpeted with pine needles. Grasses and flowers and delicate fern leaves adorned this almost sacred area. We decided to make this our camp for the night. A feeling of worship encompassed us as we went about our tasks. It seemed to me as if we had entered one of nature's private sanctuaries, reserved for all those forms of life that call the mountains home. The purity of the air itself served to purge all pollutions from within and to leave us more ready to receive than ever before. The following morning, as the sky became light above the towering pines, we broke up camp and reluctantly left after bowing our heads to give thanks for such an experience.

During the day, as we gradually made our way deeper and deeper into the mountains, following some trails and blazing others, we saw the deer, the mountain goat, the squirrel, the elk, and the tracks of many other animals.

As if visiting a friend's splendid home, we tried to partake of all the beauty around us—to look, admire, and understand the value of such precious possessions; to take nothing with us; and to leave things as nearly undisturbed as possible. The value of everything seen was enhanced because of the beauty and appreciation awakened within the heart of those who were prepared to receive what was there to share.

We saw delicate fern leaves sprinkled artistically with tiny wild flowers clustered around the bases of trees like giant Christmas tree skirts. Even the horses seemed to sense the beauty around them as they carefully picked their way one foot ahead of the other, trying, it appeared, to leave things unmolested.

Could these possibly be the same mountains that I had seen in the distance from my home over these many years I thought? *Were they those distant rugged, harsh, dominating mountains that I thought I knew so well that had been concealing their inner secrets, but were now willing to share with all those who entered reverently and stayed long enough to get acquainted and feel at peace?* In contrast to their rugged, foreboding exterior, challenging those who wished to scale the face to the top, the quiet gentle feeling from within unfolded like a trusting child eager to share.

The fifth day, in the late afternoon, we followed one another single file, obliged to trust our horses as they made their way down the narrow trail on the wet, slippery, shale rocks. It had been raining all day, and the wet shale gave way as our horses took one step and slid three, thus adding to the anxiety of this new experience.

Dad, who was in front of me, called back, "Give her the rein, Ardie and she'll be okay." It seemed that our horses sensed our precarious situation and needed a free rein to do their best.

That instruction was just opposite to the one I had been given the day before when I found myself unexpectedly caught in a swamp area with my horse Star pawing the air as the ground began sinking from under her feet. "Hold your reins tightly; keep her moving. You stay in control." That was the counsel Dad gave. Then kicking my horse's sides with my heels as vigorously as possible, I continued a rocking motion in my little English saddle and hung on tightly until my horse made a final lunge forward onto solid ground.

With care and patience, our faithful horses brought us safely down the slippery side of this shale-faced mountain. The packhorse was turned loose and, without prodding, carried our supplies safely to the bottom.

In the heart of the mountains, away from the world, there is a feeling of oneness with all living things, a love for life. Our love for each other was manifest as we shared and traded wet clothes for dry ones, with no concern for ownership. We felt gratitude for our horses that served us so well and for the wild animals that didn't seem so wild when they often peeked into our camp as if to whisper a cautious welcome.

Again, this evening, the giant conifers reached their lower branches outward and upward as if sensing our need for shelter from the rain. After unloading our packhorse, we located a large canvas tarp; and since the heavy clouds were still hanging low, we went about providing a makeshift shelter. Tying the corner of the tarp with a rope to a branch on one tree, we stretched the tarp as far as it would go in an attempt to reach the branch of another tree. The upper branches of that tree seemed to be stretching to make up the distance we needed to secure the canvas and to provide a covering overhead as rain began sprinkling again.

Crowding together under the canvas, we listened to the falling rain. Never could we have been conscious of the full aroma of the forest without the storm—as if the rain had just uncorked a giant vessel of rare perfume held in reserve for this special occasion. The smell of the smoke from the little camp fire we eventually got burning alternated with the aroma of the freshly washed forest until it became almost an intoxicating sensation, awakening my senses to feelings, smells, sights, and sounds that were new in comparison to any previous experience.

Our big Dutch oven, having been buried in the hot coals for what seemed like hours and hours, was ready to be opened. We anxiously watched as Dad carefully lifted the oven by the handle with the help of a stick and pulled it away from the fire. Everyone stood bending over, shoulder to shoulder, anticipating the condition of the contents. With the help of a smaller stick, the heavy cast-iron lid was raised just enough for all of us to take a peek. It had happened! Our bannock was now a golden brown, like one huge baking powder biscuit, filling the entire oven bottom and rounded on the top. We couldn't take it out fast enough.

This huge biscuit was carefully and quickly pulled apart in equal portions; and even while waiting for the butter and honey, I could almost taste the steam escaping from this camp fire delicacy. Never in all my eating experience has my sense of taste been so intensely keen or so completely satisfied.

That night, tucked snugly in my sleeping bag, I looked up at the towering trees above us. The rain had stopped, and the stars came out like late but welcome guests to the party that would conclude in just a few more days.

A lot of wondering goes on in the quiet of the night in the heart of the forest on a bed of pine needles with the stars dancing overhead. I just couldn't close my eyes on this most memorable day. *What if we didn't ever have another day just like this one? Would things ever in this life feel or taste or smell like this again?* And then deeper ponderings crowded in. *Why me? Here? Now? To do what? When? Where?* The questions seemed too big and the answers too remote.

"Dad," I whispered. He was in his sleeping bag right next to me.

"Yes," he answered.

"Did you know it would be like this?"

"Not exactly," he said. "There is always a bonus in nature, and this time it was the rainstorm."

"Dad," I questioned, "were you scared?"

Always honest with me, he answered, "Yes, until we got everyone off the mountain."

"But now aren't you glad it rained" I asked, wrapped comfortably inside my warm sleeping bag, the world freshly washed all around me.

"Yes," he replied.

"Me, too," I murmured. And then the stars were gone, the shadows of the mountains disappeared, the whispering of the wind in the trees quieted, and I rolled over to adjust myself better to the firm yet spongy earth mattress beneath me.

"Get up, Ardie," someone called. "We need your bed sheet for a tablecloth." I crawled out of my sleeping bag, thinking this was certainly a different standard than we had at home. I was sure Mom wouldn't approve; but with our only tablecloth still hanging wet on the line next to some of our wet clothing, and the need for a covering over the heavy dark canvas on the ground that served as our table, the use of a bed sheet seemed to be an acceptable and logical solution.

With breakfast over and everyone ready to move on, I climbed into the saddle on my faithful horse that I appreciated so much. Sharing together builds a great bond, and Star was an important part of this outstanding experience. Reluctantly we left our camp, at the same time eagerly anticipating the unfolding of a new day—a day in which each hour would bring with it a rich banquet for anyone who would partake. *Does anyone ever fully live every moment with all its offerings?* I wondered. As I tried to reach and grasp and experience the moments, I continuously became aware of so much more yet to be experienced—like one suffering indigestion from over-indulgence, I felt discomforted by my limited capacity to partake.

It was now the afternoon of the eighth day. We knew the feast was almost over as we followed the trail that led us out of the mountains near Cameron Lake. The lake was a deep emerald color, nestled like a jewel in the enclosure of a mountain retreat. A glacier in a semicircle around part of the lake enhanced the contrast of the exquisite colors. We saw many casual campers who had driven to the lake, set up their tents in which to spend the night, and cooked their meals in the conveniently located camp kitchens.

I sensed a hurting feeling inside for these people. I wanted to gather them around, one and all, take a platform stand on a tall tree stump, and call out like a transformed evangelist: "Don't live on the fringes of life when you can experience it. Don't take just a sip from the cup when a giant jug is spilling out so generously. Go deep into the forest. Stand very still in the heart of the woods and listen. Hear the snap of a twig and the wind in the trees. Discover the secrets of nature and find yourself." After I had the full attention of every camper, I would pound my fist on an imaginary pulpit and continue: "See the world as it really is, as beautiful as it was on the first day that the Lord rested. The Creator gave us our five senses and this glorious earth. The more we listen, the more we hear.

"Have you heard the water of a mountain stream gurgling like a melody down a rocky creek?

"Have you seen a spiderweb hung with dew as the sun's rays turn it into a flashing jewel?

"Have you touched the new soft, delicate, green growth on plants?

"Do you know just how many petals there are on a mountain buttercup?

"Have you nibbled on a pine needle and tasted on your lips the salt of living?

"Have you knelt on the soft earth to examine the footprints of an animal that came ahead of you and, while there, did you look up and give thanks?"

Then, lest the sermon sound too imposing, I would step down and speak softly: "Nature does not press her treasures upon us. If our hearts are open, we shall receive. When our hearts are tight within us and filled with preoccupations, we cannot receive more."

Exhausted and humbled by such an outburst, having failed to honor the insights and experiences of those campers who were perhaps even more receptive and aware than I, my heart would be quieted.

We were to return home now. A feeling of anxiousness crept over me as I anticipated the questions upon our arrival: Did you have a good time? Tell us about it. What happened? Did you have enough food? And on and on. Where do you begin when mere words become enemies to your thoughts, because words cannot adequately represent even in part an accurate accounting of what really happened?

Our mountains were never the same to me after that. Our packhorse trip had turned out to be a pilgrimage, a journey to a sacred place. It was in the mountains that I saw the sun filter through the leaves like rays of heavenly light bridging heaven and earth and casting a celestial glow that revealed only the beautiful and sacred—the majesty of all God's living things. And He was there, secluded yet very near.

From the Top of the Haystack

It was a glorious place to be—on top of the haystack right in the middle between the earth and the sky! From there we could see in all directions. Lying on our backs, my cousin and I examined all there was to see above us—the blue sky, the white, billowy clouds, and occasionally a flock of geese flying in a perfect V-shaped formation held our attention for a time. Contentment and the warm sun seemed to saturate everything. The bees seldom came that high. This private spot on top of my uncle's haystack was reserved for just a few, and invaders were seldom a problem (unless of course our voices drew the attention of our older brothers who could spoil everything).

Below us, we could survey the balance of our world. There was the clothesline just behind the house where the sheets whipped in the wind, making loud cracking sounds while losing all their wrinkles. In the winter the overalls on the line would freeze so solid that you could bring them in the house and stand them up like scarecrows until they began to thaw. Near the clothesline was the old icehouse that was filled with blocks of ice cut from the river bottom during the winter. The ice was essential for luxuries during the summer, such as homemade ice cream. It was a special day when we would make

caramel ice cream, cranking the handle on the freezer until it became harder and harder to turn, and pulling out the dasher for a healthy amount of pretesting by each of us kids.

From the top of the haystack we could see a network of narrow dirt paths leading in all directions. One led from the house to the garden, another one to the woodpile, still another to the barnyard, one more to the root cellar.

Between the clothesline and the lilac bushes was a big elm tree. It was under that tree that Colleen and I had buried a little chicken after placing it carefully in a small matchbox with handmade flannel covers and all. And in response to our pleading, Aunt LaVern had left her baking and, with flour on her apron, had stood under the tree and sang "Lead Me Gently Home," as she so often did at real funerals in our town. That happened in the springtime of the year. Now the rest of the chickens were fully grown, and we could see them below us scratching and pecking, interrupted occasionally by the proud crow of a rooster announcing his presence as a valuable member of the barnyard community.

Old Pet, the favorite horse we all liked to ride, was standing against the fence swishing her tail to keep the flies away; and the cat was lazily sunning himself on the back step of the house by the window box filled with red geraniums. The front gate, which we couldn't see from the haystack, opened out onto the gravel road leading from Colleen's house to mine; but if you could jump the ditch, the path through the open field past the cheese factory made a perfect shortcut.

On the haystack that morning we had box seats to the opening of our community drama. Like the cast in a play the townspeople seemed to be in position for the curtain to rise, and we were the audience. Mrs. Johnson was standing on a ladder, stretching full height to wash her windows which were "the cleanest in town" (anyway that's what my mom always said). Mrs. Barnes entered, the first one out with her laundry, displaying the whitest wash for which she was famous. From her own front porch Mrs. Packard was calling her children, who didn't seem to hear. On cue, people began gathering at the post office to pick up their mail. It came Mondays, Wednesdays, and Fridays; and, unless there was a lot of mail, the wicket would open around noon.

But the drama would have to continue without us. Maybe it was the aroma from the burning weeds along the ditch banks mingled with the warm sun that seemed to have such a relaxing effect. We stretched out full length in the hay to dream. *What if we had lots and lots of money?* There was a girl in our town who, we knew, was really rich. She didn't wear her worn-out Sunday dresses for school. She wore new dresses even on school days, she had her very own horse, and she had special boots just for riding.

As we lay in the straw dreaming, gradually formulating in our minds was a splendid idea—a marvelous resource was available to us that we had never even considered using before. Together we began planning what you might call a joint venture. I was somewhat accustomed to business transactions because my mom and dad owned one of the two stores in our town. It seemed as if they had everything a person could ever want in that store; and if they didn't have something they could order it from the catalogue.

On one side of the store we had groceries of all kinds, and on the other side were what Mom called the dry goods. At the back of the store were the magazines and books, and in the middle was the hardware (nails, bolts and hammers), and rubber boots hung from a rack overhead. I don't remember where everything was located, but I know there were luxuries and necessities galore: coal oil, mouse seed (poison), laying mash, gasoline, vinegar, flour, liniment, fine china, ladies' dresses and shoes, and an entire glass showcase filled with a variety of candies— licorice and suckers of every kind. Over the years I had watched people come to the store week after week with money to buy goods outright or to offer butter or eggs and sometimes other commodities in exchange for whatever they wanted.

Now, from the top of the haystack, our plan for financial

independence began to unfold. We climbed carefully down through the hayloft in the barn and made our way to Colleen's chicken coop. Trying not to disturb the hens, we moved from one to another reaching under their feathery bodies into the warm nest in search of an egg or two. With one brown egg for each of us, we headed toward the store.

By the time we arrived at the store, there were many customers who had come from the post office just across the street to get some groceries before returning home. This "busy time," as Mom used to call it, was to the advantage of Colleen and myself.

I decided to handle the business transaction by myself while Colleen waited outside. Taking both eggs, I slipped in the front door and casually made my way to a large egg crate on the opposite side of the store from where Mom was waiting on customers. I carefully placed the two brown eggs in the wooden crate with dividers, which looked like a large icecube tray with a piece of cardboard between each layer, and quickly walked away. At just the right time I removed two chocolate-covered torpedo suckers from the case, put them in front of me, and left the store through the back room.

Colleen met me by the corner, and we headed back toward the haystack to enjoy our investment and continue our daydreaming. Our unlimited resources seemed very promising. And as long as the chickens kept laying, we knew we could match our wants with our opportunities.

That evening after the store was closed, Mom came in the house and said she wanted to talk to me. I had a funny feeling in my stomach as she called me to her side. "It's about the eggs," she said. "Where did you get them?"

How did she know? I wondered. *Who told her?* But I said: "We didn't steal them, Mom. We got them from Colleen's chickens. They were her eggs."

"Her eggs?" Mom questioned.

"We needed some money," I continued, "and I didn't have any. You give other people things for eggs. We just traded. I put the eggs in the crate," I explained.

"Well," Mom continued, "if you need money, we had better provide a way for you to get it."

Mom always had a way of working things out to the satisfaction of her customers, and this suggestion sounded promising to me. I had never before had any "money coming in" (a phrase I had often heard from customers who arranged to get groceries without money). Instead of paying, those customers had things written on a bill which was filed in a metal box until a later time. Some arrangements were more challenging than others but, as I remember, a satisfactory agreement was always achieved.

There was the time, however, that old Brother Burns brought a small basket of butter in to make an exchange. His request was different than usual though—he wanted to exchange butter for butter. "You see, the Missus found a mouse in our cream. But it hasn't hurt the butter," he explained as he removed the little white napkin that covered it. "It looks just like any other butter." And it did look the same, since everyone who made butter used the same brand of butter paper that they bought from our store and the same size mold. He continued, "If you didn't know, it would taste just the same."

With a rightful sense of propriety, Mom tried to explain the inappropriateness of such an exchange, but her reasoning was unconvincing. The man with the butter, who was the only customer in the store, stood on one side of the counter unrelenting in his bargaining efforts, and Mom stood on the other side. "But there is no difference," he insisted.

Convinced that he could see no difference, Mom took his basket of butter to the back room where our fridge was located and carefully unpacked his few pounds of butter from the basket. With equal care she rearranged the same butter in the basket, replacing the little white covering. This customer, like most other customers, left smiling with the satisfaction of a favorable business transaction!

I was anxious now to hear what Mom had in mind to take care of my financial deficiency. She and Dad must have discussed this situation, and come to an agreement because Mom explained to me that from that day on I was to have money coming in. They called it an allowance, explaining that with an allowance came specific responsibilities and duties. The arrangement was made and agreed upon by all parties concerned. The contract was written on paper. We all signed our names and Grandma, who was living with us, affixed her name to the document as a witness to this official arrangement.

With money in my hand and more coming in, my wants ran in all direction like pigs released from a pen. By the end of the week my money, which had seemed so limitless, was gone, and it was yet another week before payday. Like bread rising in a pan, my needs got bigger and bigger, while my income was fixed by contract.

My experience in helping in the store was teaching me many things about economics, and I was ready for the next adventure. One morning as Mom was unpacking the bread and putting it neatly on the shelf, I approached my subject with the seriousness of any customer. "Mom," I said, "can I have some credit?"

She looked up from her task and questioned, "What do you mean, my dear?"

I wasn't sure exactly what I meant, but I had heard customers say that and it seemed to work like money. They went ahead and got what they wanted. And instead of putting their money in the till, they just wrote what they got on a bill and Mom filed it away. There was another way that seemed to work almost as well. I remembered that the Indians would bring their beautiful beaded buckskin moccasins, and some-times even a jacket, to "leave them in soak," as they called it. They could get the groceries they wanted, and we would hold their things until their treaty checks came at the end of the month. Then they would drive to town in their wagons, with the whole family in their colorful skirts and blankets and always a dog or two following behind, to cash their checks, pay their bills, reclaim their possessions, and buy some more goods.

Old Rough Hair, with his long white braids tied with colorful ribbon, would struggle with his gnarled fingers to take his check from the envelope, turn it over, and haltingly mark a big X to serve as his signature, as most of the other Indians did.

Since I had nothing to leave in soak, I felt that a request for credit was my best approach. Mom explained that she only gave credit to people who were out of money, who had some money coming in, and who could be trusted. I was excited. I knew I qualified, yet she still seemed hesitant.

"If you get in the habit of overspending your allowance, my dear," she explained, "you can get into serious trouble. You know," she continued, "when I give credit to some of our Indian customers and they sign their checks over to me, they no longer have any choice about what they can do with their checks. They are no longer free to spend their money as they wish."

"But, Mom," I insisted, "I'll give my allowance back to you."

I must have been as persuasive as Brother Burns was with the butter transaction, because she agreed to extend credit and trust me. She prepared an official bill with my name on the top and placed it in the file.

The days slipped by as my appetite for many possessions continued. My attention to the things I had purchased was of little consequence compared to the intensity of my desire for what I yet wanted.

Finally it was payday again and Mom counted out my allowance into my waiting hand, and just as casually she took the bill from the file and handed it to me. Somehow, at that moment, it didn't seem fair.

"But, Mom," I protested. She just held out her hand, much as I had done a moment before. I reluctantly counted most of my hard-earned money back into her hand. She put the money in the till, marked the bill "paid in full," and handed it to me. Looking at the bill and then at Mom, my feeling of anxiety began to mount.

"But, Mom, what will I do when we go to the rodeo in Cardston next week? I hardly have any money left." I knew I couldn't get credit for cotton candy and a ride on the ferris wheel, and the rodeo and midway only came to town once a year.

"But, my dear," Mom tried to explain, "you made that choice when you asked for credit; and once you spend your money for one thing, the money is gone and you are no longer free to choose what you will do with that money. The time you spend earning that money will not return and neither will the choices for that money."

"But, Mom," I explained, now feeling completely frustrated, "with so many things to want, how can you choose?"

She just smiled. "You'll learn."

I wished then that I didn't even have an allowance. I had liked it better when Mom took care of it all. After ten cents was taken out of every dollar for tithing, I didn't seem to have much left anyway.

My economic future looked bleak but, as with other customers in a financial bind, Mom came to my rescue. "I'll tell you what I'll do," she said. "I think we can work this out." I listened eagerly. "If you would like to wash all the shelves in the store as far up as you can reach, I will give you a five-dollar advance besides one dollar spending money in addition to your regular allowance." The solution came so quickly that I immediately felt relieved and hurriedly agreed to the arrangement.

My dad took my friends and me to the rodeo. He bought our tickets to the midway and also bought our lunches. I spent my dollar on cotton candy, a balloon, a ride on the ferris wheel, and other things. And then I saw a display of little glass balls with tiny snow scenes encased in the glass. When I shook the ball, the snow would fall heavily until the storm was over and then I could shake it again. I had never seen anything like this before. I gave the lady my money and took my treasure. It was a glorious day.

The next day I began my project of washing shelves. I started in the corner with all the little things—the Mercurochrome, the aspirins, the liniment, the adhesive tape, and all the other items that took so much time to move. The cans of carbolic salve had rounded corners and kept tipping over. I was so glad when my hour had passed.

The following day I tackled the bread and cereal shelves which weren't too bad, but one hour is a long time—especially if someone is waiting for you to go and play.

On Saturday I didn't even want to get out of bed. Besides my regular duties, I had to do some more shelves. This time it was the shelves displaying the cans of jam and syrup, honey and molasses. Reluctantly, I went to the store and began the job. Some of the cans had stuck to the shelf. The black on the shelves from the bottom of the cans just wouldn't come off. That day, I scrubbed and scrubbed. My hands were in the water so long my fingers became wrinkled like prunes.

I knew two things—I didn't like credit, and I didn't ever want an advance again. Nothing I could think of was worth the burden of this monumental job unless it was to buy back my freedom, and I had already exchanged that. There just had to be a better way!

One day, weeks later, as I lay alone on my stomach on top of Dad's haystack, I imagined what it would be like to have my own pony right there in the pasture below. I closed my eyes and could feel myself riding at full speed the three miles to our farm and back, with the wind on my face and blowing my hair. Other dreams also crowded in and then slipped away as I became interested in watching the Hutterites who had parked in front of our store. They didn't usually bring their children to town with them, but this day three young girls in long, black dresses and checkered head scarves waited in one of the trucks.

The Hutterites lived in a colony just across the river. They had acres and acres of grain and worked very hard. They would haul their grain to the elevators and would receive payment by check. Then, wearing dark suits and black hats, they would

come into town to our store to cash their checks. By special arrangement Mom was bonded as a paying agent. Once a week she and Dad would make the twenty-mile trip to pick up money for these wealthy grain growers. These hundreds of dollars were kept in a metal box in the big steel safe in the office of our store. Once the dial on the safe was turned, there was no way of getting into it. Only Mom and Dad knew the combination.

There on the haystack I pondered all the choices the Hutterites could make with all that money. It was right then that I began considering a different approach to my economic program. The Hutterites returned to their trucks, the big pockets in their black pants bulging with envelopes full of money, and drove off. I slid down the low side of my dream castle and headed for the store. I approached Mom and made my proposal. "Mom," I said, "I would like to have an envelope for my money in that metal box in the safe. Okay?" She agreed.

From that day on, along with the Hutterites, I had an envelope in the safe. Gradually, as my ability to make wise choices improved, my envelope began to fill up—not as much as the Hutterites yet; but, when considering the possibility from the vantage point of the haystack, given enough time even this seemed within reach.

The thrill of saving for bigger things became more rewarding than spending for little things, and I learned yet another lesson in economics. My brother needed a loan, and on that occasion my grandmother told me about interest. An agreement was made, Grandma witnessed the note, and my brother used my money. On the appointed date he paid back the loan, plus interest. This arrangement became very exciting to me, and I looked for other opportunities to repeat the procedure.

Just before my fourteenth birthday I made the biggest business deal of all. Dad had known for some time how desperately I wanted a horse. A couple of weeks before my birthday he explained to me that he had seen a pony he thought we could be interested in. He said it would cost quite a bit, but

45

we could buy one together if I were interested. The questions my parents had asked so many times before were once again repeated: "Are you sure that's what you want? Are you willing to pay the price?"

I was sure I wanted a pony and I was willing, even anxious, to pay the price if it could be arranged. Taking my envelope that was now bulging with money from its safe place in the metal box, I sat with Mom and Dad to count our combined resources. Together, it appeared to me as if we were free to buy whatever we wanted in the whole world.

On Wednesday we went to the horse auction in Lethbridge. Dad had previously inquired and had an idea about which horse would be best for us. We waited and watched for quite a while until the auctioneer in his rapid, repetitive, colorful lingo called out for anyone interested in what I knew just had to be our horse. My heart pounded against my chest until it was hard to breathe. Several people indicated an interest and began bidding. Dad spoke right up and made his bid. The amount bid was less than our combined assets. The auctioneer called a higher amount, and someone raised a hand. This happened several times. It was almost too hard to watch. Finally, Dad called out an even higher price. I thought I would explode before the auctioneer finally responded to Dad's last and highest bid by dropping his hand as he pointed in our direction. "Sold!" he said.

The pony with the white star on her forehead was ours. I grabbed Dad and jumped up and down. We hugged each other. "She's ours!" I shouted.

"No," Dad replied, "she's yours! Yours because you saved your money, and together we could pay the highest price."

"For which of you," asked the Savior, "intending to build a tower, sitteth not down first, and counteth the cost, whether he have sufficient to finish it?" (Luke 14:28.)

The
Undertow

To most newcomers it would appear that little or nothing happened in our quiet little village on the prairie. But the townspeople boasted of their stores (both of them), the post office, the gas station, the church, and the school, of course; and they took pride in their brightly painted homes sprinkled sparingly throughout the village proper. Near the west edge of town tall grain elevators stood like beacons on the prairie, towering high above the skyline as, we imagined, the Empire State Building might do in the big faraway city that we had heard about.

To the eyes of the villagers, especially the young, the town was not in hibernation at all (as it might appear to the outsider), but was actually teeming with activities, most of them of our own making. On a stormy day when the harsh temperature required that we remain indoors, we would thumb through the magazines and talk about the lucky kids in the big cities with all their rich opportunities and advantages and their variety of exciting activities. Then from our limited vantage point we would contemplate: *Without open fields, quiet meadows, and crystal clear streams to explore, where do the city kids go for fun anyway?* Maybe too many choices would just get in the way, we would often console ourselves.

Except in the winter when the roads were snowbound, the mail, which came three times a week, included the catalogues and other magazines that kept us in touch with the glamour of the world that we often recreated in our play. Our long summer days were filled with a greater variety of activities. Bringing the cows in from the pasture for milking in the late afternoon almost became a ritual. Walking along the narrow dirt path bordered high on either side with tall grass and sweet clover, watching the bees darting in and out among the buffalo beans and wild roses, my good friend and I would share all our important thoughts as we followed lazily behind the cows that knew their way home. On these occasions the dreams of the big city were as far away as the cities themselves, and everything important was within our reach.

Old Jersey always took the lead in this daily parade, and the other cows would follow. On the days I went to the pasture alone, she would stand by the fence while I climbed on her back to take the easy way home. Old Jersey was like one of our family, and I was even more willing to defend that cow than I was a family member in disputes about qualities or worthwhile attributes. Occasionally the opportunity for defense presented itself.

One evening after my friend and I had followed the cows back to the pasture and I was closing the gate, she announced that her dad's holstein cows were better than my dad's jersey cows. This probably was my first experience in the art of serious debate. With the facts clearly and emphatically presented, my explaining that my dad's cows gave less milk but more cream did not seem to compensate in my friend's mind for the fact that her dad's cows gave more milk but less cream. To that argument I attempted to explain that less cream meant not as rich and therefore not as good either. That, of course, increased the intensity of our debate, which lasted, I must confess, during the better part of our growing-up years. I guess

she never really did accept the obvious fact that jersey cows are better than holsteins.

During our growing years we had many lessons to learn, and our prairie home seemed to provide them in constant regularity.

One summer, the year of my eighth birthday, a young girl named Lorraine came from Victoria, British Columbia, to spend a couple of weeks with her aunt. Lorraine's clothes were fancy—they all matched. And she always wore a special perfume that served to increase my desire for the nice things from the city. I later learned, however, that the smell I had so much enjoyed wasn't perfume at all, but rather mosquito repellent that her mother had sent along to protect her from an environment to which she was unaccustomed. It was well that Lorraine wore that "perfume" too, because swimming in the river was one of our prairie rituals, and mosquitos were often invaders of our ceremonial dips.

It was the Saturday evening at the Belly River down by the big bridge that my friends and I relished as one of our rich opportunities. Sometimes sharing important things with other is like seeing those things for the first time in renewed splendor. And so it was as my friends Colleen, Nita, Doreen, Connie and I stood on the bank together explaining to Lorraine, our newfound friend from the city, about the majesty of our river. Dad, I remember, stood quietly back allowing us the full responsibility of defending with pride and loyalty our village and all of its assets. As if by magic the river took on new charm in my eyes. In a sudden display of beauty, the rapids, the pier, and the big bridge (which had immediately increased in size and grandeur) seemed now, I thought, equal to any city sights to which our friend might be making a comparison.

We all played follow the leader to our private spot in the trees where we made a quick change into our swimming suits. As Lorraine began folding her clothes after getting into her fancy swimming suit, we explained the convenience of the branches which served as hangers and provided a quick demonstration by hurriedly tossing our clothes onto the limbs which held them until our return.

I don't recall ever going a second time to the river with Lorraine. On the way home she said something about the gravel hurting her bare feet, the coldness of the water (which she even said was dirty!), and I don't remember what else— maybe it was something about the mosquitos but she didn't return to the river and I don't think she ever came back to see her aunt after that summer. But we returned to the river many, many times.

I guess I can't blame Lorraine for not enjoying our river. I remember the first time I went swimming. It took a lot of courage to walk out to the very edge of that narrow pier jutting out into the deep water and then to jump off, but that's where we all began. As I recall now, the courage to hold my breath, hold my nose, and jump into that great expanse came as I looked above me to the left of the pier where the bigger kids were jumping from the high steel bridge. Those kids, including my brother, seemed to be fearless as they jumped from the high level into the water below.

In our town the older kids usually charted the course for the younger ones, and we all followed. It had been that way for years—not only in swimming and jumping, but in everything else we thought important. Folks in the community knew and often spoke of the hometown boy who became a famous doctor and worked at the Mayo Clinic, and the girl who became a specialist as a nurse, and many others. They too as children had jumped off the pier, and many of them off the bridge. It was almost as though that early childhood experience marked the first of all the challenges that led them to greater and greater victories, and that we were all expected to follow.

As I stood looking down at the water below on my first attempt to jump from the pier, the question was never *if* I would jump but rather *when*, and that seemed to be resolved when someone with more courage (since it wasn't her turn) urged me from behind. Except for the important fact that my father was in the water below with his arms outstretched and waiting, not knowing how to swim and never having heard of a life jacket made the whole experience very frightening. While anxiously measuring the distance over the end of the pier to the water below, I sensed, several times in succession, a scary feeling bubble up inside and then quiet down, until from deep within a feeling of something taking over caused me to close my eyes, hold my nose and my breath in preparation, and then take the big jump that I knew was inevitable.

A chorus of loud cheers went up on that occasion, the memory of which resounds in my ears even yet; and over the years those cheers from the hometown folk have been like echoes in the canyon of the soul. They have become a part of the reservoir of courage for the bigger jumps that have followed.

I came up out of the water just as Dad said I would. He lifted me high above his head while trying to keep me from climbing all over him in my urgent need to cling to something secure. Brushing the wet hair from my face, I listened for his quiet response. His approval was never too loud or showy, lest we rest too much on the victory without being ready for the next challenge. "Good try," he said. "Let's do it again."

After I had made several tries, as I recall, and with little or no hesitation at the edge of the pier except to make sure that someone was watching to provide an audience, Dad delayed my performance long enough to explain. "This time when you come up, I'll be right here. But I won't take your hands. You'll need both of them to keep yourself above water." He continued his instruction. "Just keep paddling and kicking, and I will be right by you." I listened to all of the instructions, and because I knew he'd be there I dared to try. I heard again in my mind, "I'll be right by you." And he was—again and again, time after time, until several summers had passed and I could jump and swim quite well.

Now I began to feel confident even without Dad being along, especially since he had provided what he called a self-reliance measure in case I got caught in the rapids or encountered some other emergency. He had taught me to flip over on my back and float downstream if I became tired or found myself in difficulty, and I would float like that just long enough to catch my breath before trying again. We practiced this together many times until even the rapids became less of a challenge. With my increasing confidence, Dad's part in our summer activity actually seemed quite unnecessary. But we could reach the river quicker by riding the three miles with him in his car than we could by fighting the gravel road on our bikes.

I recall how we savored every warm day as a bonus as we reluctantly watched the daylight hours shorten and yield to the coming fall. Toward the end of the summer of my tenth year, my dad, his friend, and I took some time off from the harvesting for a swim. As Dad always said, "If we need an excuse we have to take time to bathe anyway and this is as good a way as any." He had brought a bar of soap and some shampoo to support his argument. To me, this swim was the luxury that followed a day of hard work.

On this occasion it was more convenient for us to go to a river on the other side of town, but this only increased my anticipation for our swim. With my suit already on I jumped out of the car and ran for the inviting water. Dad and his friend headed toward the trees to change. That was okay with me—I felt that I could manage quite well by myself.

The water was cool and inviting, making me anxious to go in deeper. It wasn't the river I was used to, but I had no concerns until I was a few yards from shore. Then I felt an unfamiliar, frightening current around me. Increasing in its intensity, the water became a strong force trying to suck me under. I struggled against it. A frantic sensation engulfed me as the undertow from which I couldn't escape seemed to exceed my strength. I tried to shout, "Dad! Dad!"

Looking toward the shore, I saw him running toward me shouting: "Listen to me! Do you hear? You can make it! Do

what I tell you!" I don't remember seeing him again before I went under the water, but I could hear his voice in my mind: "Do what I tell you!" And then from somewhere came his clear instruction: "Keep swimming and head for the big tree. You can make it!" Over and over in my mind I heard his simple instruction and kept trying until finally the force of the current seemed to relinquish its victim, and I was released in calmer water. Exhausted and weak, again I heard my father's voice, "Flip over on your back and float."

Had I not heard his voice, in my frightened and weakened condition I might have forgotten the self-reliance measure he had taught me. I responded to his counsel automatically, and the river immediately carried me downstream until some branches near the water's edge held me captive. While waiting in those tangled branches, shivering probably from fear, since the water was not that cold, I could hear my father's voice as he ran toward me: "You're okay. We'll make it!" Releasing me from the branches and pulling me from the water, he wrapped my frightened, trembling body in his arms as I began to cry.

What would have happened without my father, I thought. *What if I hadn't heard his voice, and what if I hadn't followed?*

Never again did I return to that river to swim, but over the years those same questions have returned again and again to my mind—What if I hadn't heard his voice? What if I hadn't followed?

"And while I was thus struggling in the spirit, behold, the voice of the Lord came into my mind." (Enos 10.)

Grandmother's House on the Prairie

In the heart of our town were two large two-story twin houses built by twin brothers Edward and Edwin, who married Nellie and Nettie. One house was located on the northeast corner of the block and the other one on the southeast corner. While the houses, like their owners, appeared identical on the outside, there were notable differences within. It was the house on the northeast corner that I came to know well—the one owned by Edwin Leavitt, my grandfather.

The old house with its fancy porches, big pillars and gabled roof, still wearing much of its charm of years past, was set back off the street and partially secluded on three sides by drooping branches of the sheltering cottonwood trees. Coming up the path and passing through the front door, one could sense the entrance into a world of endless adventure. There were many rooms on the three levels: the parlor, the sitting room, the pantry, the pump room, the wardrobe closet, the veranda on the second floor, the basement, and all the rooms in between. But it was not the number of rooms or their varying sizes that made the house so exciting; more important was the drama that unfolded within. The walls of that dwelling enclosed secrets and joys and memories never to be erased.

Bordering the house on one side was a row of caragana bushes heavily laden with little green pods. These pods became the official currency in our play store located on the south veranda. From the veranda we could lean out and pick the pods from the top of the tall bushes and have ready-made "cash" for our store. From the veranda we could also look down on the straight rows of deep red and pink peonies, the pansy bed, white peonies planted inside the big tractor wheel. The wheel was right in the middle of the lawn (I had fallen over it and received a bad cut on my lip while running one day with a blanket over my head).

A dirt path packed with cinders from the coal-burning furnace led from the front gate by the ditch to a large porch that provided an impressive entrance to my grandparents' home. Bolted onto the first step of the porch was the old mud-scraper. On rainy days we would hold onto a pillar with one hand while attempting to scrape off the thick, claylike mud that clung to our overshoes or rubbers like glue, making our feet appear at least twice their normal size.

The front door opened to a large entrance hall dominated by the beautifully carved wooden staircase leading to the second floor. The first door on the left of the entrance hall was usually closed and had an official-looking sign which read, "Walk In." This room had a big window, a high ceiling, brightly flowered wallpaper, and a floral design in the shiny linoleum on the floor. There was a coal stove near the center of the room and a rod behind the door for hanging coats. Next to the window was the switchboard.

The switchboard was the heart of the communications system in our town for all those who had telephones. For those who didn't, my cousins and I were often employed during the summer months to take a message notifying the person without a telephone that he was to call the operator because someone wanted to talk to him. The charge for this service was ten cents unless it was stormy, and then the person being called was asked to pay an additional five cents for the added inconvenience.

We children were informed that the equipment in this room was government property, and there was to be no misconduct in or around the telephone office either during or after hours. The office opened at eight in the morning and closed at eight in the evening. People could not use their telephones outside of these hours, and the switchboard was then left unattended. It did have an emergency alarm that could signal my grandmother from any part of this big house in case of emergency, and then by special arrangement a call could be put through after hours.

One evening after eight P.M. when the office was closed, the possibility of responding to what seemed to be an emergency took hold of my cousin and me. We knew, as did almost everyone else in the town, that Bill Bradley and Sarah Coombs (whose romance had once enlivened the interest and conversation of everyone for months) had now come to an abrupt halt. It was a known fact that due to some serious misunderstanding Bill had publicly refused to speak to Sarah unless she spoke to him first. And Sarah, with the pride of her family heritage, resolved never to speak to Bill if it depended on her speaking first. This large switchboard, now standing idle, suggested to us the possibility of resolving a serious dilemma.

The switchboard resembled a tall box with a shelf in the front. The operator sat on a high stool and wore an earpiece (held in place with a wire band fitting over the head and around the neck) and a black horn-shaped piece that she spoke into. In front of her on the switchboard were many plugs with long cords. There were also rows and rows of holes that the plugs were pushed into, depending on who wanted to talk to whom.

My grandmother would interview and hire "responsible young women" in our town to work the shifts from eight A.M. to eight P.M. I loved to watch the operators and listen to them say "Number please" and then, with the speed of lightning plug one cord in, and with a flip of the wrist pull another one out at the signal (a tiny plate that dropped) when the conversation was over. In private I practiced over and over saying, "Number, please," and "Just a moment, please," trying to get the twang and the very same inflection in my voice so that I would sound like an official telephone operator.

The moment of preparation, opportunity, and need loomed before us. Just after eight P.M. my cousin and I, unauthorized except for our righteous desire to do good, slipped quietly through the back bedroom and entered the phone office through the small door by the closet. We agreed that we were to share in this deed, whether it be honorable or otherwise. There was a headset for each of us. I climbed onto the stool and my accomplice stood close by.

Our plan would only work if both parties were at home, but we decided to take the chance. I pushed a plug into the hole for the Bradley residence, rang a long and two shorts, and then waited. "Hello?" I heard. Luck was with us—it was Bill. Then sounding as official as my practice would allow, I said, "Just a moment, please." Then my cousin put the other plug in place, rang three shorts, and waited. Our plan was working. It was Sarah who answered this time. "Hello," she said. Again I tried for that official inflection in my voice. "Just a moment, please," I replied.

My cousin pushed the switch forward connecting the two parties who had vowed never to speak to each other, and just like an official operator I said, "Go ahead, please."

Both parties spoke at once, "Hello?" Then somewhat confused and not sure who was calling, since both were speaking at the same time, they repeated, "Hello?"

Sarah then asked, "Were you calling me?"

Bill, now aware of who was calling and wanting to set the record straight, with a tone of joy in his voice in place of the hurting that must have been there responded, "No, you called me."

Sarah, confident that it was not she who had called, and obviously relieved by the communication, attempted to ease the situation by admitting that it really didn't matter who called first anyway.

My cousin and I covered our mouths to keep from making any sound that would attract attention to our unauthorized use of government property.

After that, people began inquiring about the renewed romance, wanting to know who really spoke first. To my knowledge no answer was ever given. It remained a secret within the walls of Grandma's wonderful house.

While the phone office was not a place for children to play, Grandmother always said we were welcome in any other room in the house; and some places were especially designated for our enjoyment. Under the central stairway was a little place like a tiny house of our own. The ceiling was slanted, and on one side of this little narrow room were storage shelves laden with boxes and oversized pots and pans. On one of the shelves in the corner was a large oatmeal box which was always filled with large, round sugar cookies just for us. I can't ever remember the box being empty. That little room with the light bulb hanging down from a cord in the center was warm and cozy and quiet; we would sit inside talking and sharing secrets for hours. The room had a special smell—sort of a dusty smell, but I liked it.

On the other side of the kitchen and through the pantry was the pump room. This room was filled with a wonderful smell like wet moss and tree bark. One pull of the pump handle released cool, sparkling water that would pour out of the mouth of the pump into the white enamel basin on the cabinet.

When the whole family came for dinner and the house was filled with aunts and uncles and cousins there were also lots of dishes to do. If we thought we might be pressed into service, my cousins and I would escape to the pump room and lock the door. Here we were safe unless someone wanted us—in which case the pump room was always the first place they looked.

The other place they might have checked on but never did, was the wardrobe closet by the bedroom. It wasn't a closet that was used frequently. It was more of a storage closet, filled with heavy winter coats, boots, scarves, gloves, old clothes, and worn-out overalls that were saved "in case of hard times." In that closet there was no light, and no end, as far as I had discovered. You could be lost there from everyone. But I never wanted to get lost that much. I went in it just once while playing hide and seek. I don't know if I became frightened because I didn't know how far back the closet went, or if I just got scared trying to push my way through all the heavy clothes that seemed to smother me. But I made a quick decision: I would rather be caught than ever hide in that place again.

On the second story of the house at the front were the bedrooms. When sleeping over, we would be tucked into a cozy, wonderful, soft bed. Each child was covered with a light feather tick that made him feel as if he were nestled under a blanket of feathers. A kiss good night and the lingering smell of Grandma's lilac dusting powder always brought a perfect ending to the day.

There were some spare rooms on the top floor that were used for storage. One room in particular provided a service to the community. My cousins and I never went near that room, though we dared each other many times. In that room, we knew, was a stack of wooden caskets of various sizes made by some men in the Church. When someone died and a casket was needed, the sisters would then turn the wooden box into a beautiful satin-lined bed with a soft feathery mattress.

While my cousins and I stayed clear of that room, my brother and his cousins dared each other to sleep all night in one of those wooden caskets. One time several of the boys decided they would do it, as each one refused to be outdone by the other. They all vowed to remain the entire night. To make the experience more memorable, unbeknown to the boys our Uncle Ted lay down in one of the boxes, pulled a white sheet over himself, fitted the lid in place, and waited. The boys came into the room much less boisterous than they had been when they first made the dare. Uncle Ted waited for their imaginations to reach their peak before he quietly and very slowly rose up out of the casket. The boys evacuated that room,

their feet hardly touching the floor. No one ever slept there after that.

The kitchen was located right in the center of this big house, and it seemed as if Grandma baked every day—at least the smell of hot bread, scones, and mince pies was always present in that part of the house. The round oak table was covered with a sparkling white oilcloth that could be wiped clean after each meal, and in the center of the table was a deep cutglass bowl with the handles of teaspoons sticking out of the top.

After finishing his bread and milk topped with big lumps of thick cream and sugar, Grandpa would often pause and lean back, balancing on the legs of his chair until I was afraid he would topple over. Resting his thumbs in the sides of his overalls, he would brag about his great successes with crops and grandchildren, saying that he had never had a failure. I knew that an early frost had ruined many of the crops one year, and so this claim appeared to me to be a question of honesty and it weighed heavily on my mind.

I asked Dad about this matter once. "Well, you see," Dad explained, "your Grandfather refuses to ever be discouraged with crops or grandchildren. He sees no flaws in either, and in his mind he makes up the necessary adjustment with faith in the future. You might call it optimistic miscalculation." It was not until several years later, when I saw Grandpa's unwavering faith in a grandchild that some might have classified as a crop failure, that I better accepted his way of figuring.

Next to the kitchen was the parlor, with its high ceiling and long, narrow windows and beautiful lace curtains. In the corner was a fancy china closet with convex glass doors. It was filled with colorful, odd-shaped little dishes—an orange-colored mustard dish with a hand-painted scene on it, and a tiny white ladle that fit through the hole in the top; a pickle dish of burgundy red glass; and a pair of milk glass saltshakers shaped like little chickens. We would take these treasures out very carefully and admire them and "speak for" them after

Grandma died. There seemed to be no relationship between our interest in the dishes and the passing of Grandma. Choosing was just a way of identifying our favorite treasure.

Just across the room was the large furnace grate recessed in the floor. The little square holes let the hot air from the coal furnace below rise up in a mighty effort to heat the whole house. In the wintertime, especially on Sunday afternoons, Grandma would sit in her rocking chair near the furnace grate and my cousins and I would stand right in the middle of the grate, feeling the flow of the hot air. The metal on our garters (used to hold up our heavy wool stockings) would get so hot that we hardly dared move for fear the garters would touch our legs and burn us. We had the idea that if we could absorb enough heat, it would stay with us longer when we went out into the Canadian winter.

While we absorbed as much heat as possible, Grandma would tell us our favorite stories over and over again. She told us about "Singing Jessee" and "Old Raggles" and stories that made us cry and want to be better. Once away from that favored location the intensity of the heat quickly diminished and there seemed to be no way of storing a surplus for future use. Reluctantly leaving the warmth of the room, we anxiously awaited the next opportunity to be warmed clear through.

Over the years we became experts at finding our way through every room in the big house, but it is the warmth from the hours spent at Grandmother's side that guides us even yet through less familiar paths.

Waiting for the Day

In all the days of my life I had never felt more excited or full of anticipation than I did that spring. The season which had been so long in coming was now finally edging its way forward as each month we anxiously tore a page from the big calendar that hung in the kitchen by the old wall telephone.

I knew that the crocuses, still hidden under a slowly melting blanket of snow, were pushing upward against the cold earth until the day they would break through their winter protection into the warm sunshine and announce the approaching season. The furry squirrels, the birds, the baby lambs, the calves, the little pigs, the turkeys, and all other forms of life, though not yet visible, I somehow knew were keeping pace on their own particular time schedule and would be ready to answer "Present" to nature's roll call and to play an important part in this great event.

The buds on the trees were enlarging in answer to the coaxing of the warm sun. There were shooting stars, the buffalo beans, the sweet clover and the larkspur. It was as if each section in the large symphony of nature was responding to the entrance cues of a great conductor while spring made her almost furtive arrival, until one day the entire orchestra would

burst forth with a grand tutti passage in full bloom and majestic glory.

But I especially loved the glorious feeling of cool, fresh air on bare legs after a long season of itchy wooly socks that were supposed to be a welcome protection against the harsh and stinging temperatures of the winter. In my younger years I had always rushed this glorious fresh-air experience that was so much a part of spring. Unknown to my parents, of course, after I had passed the corner by the garage and the picket gate in front of Aunt Ione's house, I would turn my back to the world, unfasten my cumbersome garters, and then roll my long stockings down until they looked like giant doughnuts encircling both ankles just above shoes now freed from their heavy winter boots. With bare legs exposed to that glorious cool breeze, I knew spring had arrived and felt sorry for those kids who had to wait until it was warm enough (to make sure they wouldn't catch cold) before experiencing this memorable sensation. Maybe I would catch cold, I thought. But that uncertain possibility could never outweigh the well-known sensation that causes the fuzz on your legs to stand up and the thousands of pores on the skin to be awakened after a long sleep.

Each spring the fresh-air feeling told me that I was really alive. And with restored strength in my "new" legs, now freed from those burdensome stockings, it seemed as though I could run faster and jump the ditches easier than before. In fact, the only thing worse than the stockings themselves was contending with the pantywaist (which was some sort of a harness used to keep the stockings up). This problem, however, was also minimized after I discovered that leaving my stockings on under my pajamas saved me from having to untangle them each morning—an operation that took an unreasonable period of time, especially when there came the reiterated reminders from Mom in the kitchen, "Hurry, you're going to be late!"

Several springs had come and gone since the beginning of what I considered my fresh-air ritual, and those experiences slipped away, making room for moments of even greater anticipation. This particular spring I would not have traded my place on earth for that of any other living thing. It had been like waiting for the gong of midnight on New Year's Eve. The unshakable order and perfect timing of nature was about to deliver another season—this one so long in coming was reserved unquestionably for me.

The warming of the early sun may sometimes have been delayed, but there was never any variation in the sequence of the cycle that repeated itself over and over in constant regularity—spring, summer, fall, and winter. And each and every season, like a faithful schoolmaster, had brought its own variety of lessons to be presented to the not-always-eager learner. But even with reluctant students nature has a way of penetrating the mind to ensure a lasting lesson.

It was during the summer that I had begun anticipating with increased interest the arrival of this spring and all the events that would follow. During our catch-up time (those weeks between planting and harvesting) my dad spent considerable time with the other farmers discussing the weather, the moisture, the drying winds, the dust storms, the hailstorms, and the terrible recollection of the premature frost that had come after two seasons of drought back in 1931—just as if talking about the weather might in some way help control its behavior.

During that summer I walked side by side with Dad almost daily through some section of our eighty acres. As soon as the grain was visible above the ground, I found myself anxiously sensing the high risk and the high stakes involved in farming, and I became more aware of the importance of a full growing season with ample time for the grain to mature if we were to have a good harvest. I became very worried and deeply concerned with the threat of a hailstorm, an early frost, or too much moisture too late that might cut short the precious growing season. I also became aware for the first time that we had to pay the bank for the loan to buy the seed that we had so carefully selected and planted at just the right time. But, then, on the other hand, I enjoyed speculating with Dad about our possible surplus if the growing season were not cut short and the heads of the grain ripened to full maturity, every kernel in every head, to ensure a bumper crop, as Dad called it.

Our future looked very bright that year, but I had learned that Dad always took every precaution available to reduce as much as possible any risk factor. Then he put his "trust in a kind Providence to manage the rest."

The snow was still piled high around the eaves of our house that morning as I jumped out of bed and ran to the kitchen, pulling the month of February from the calendar. There it was right before my eyes—March, the first day. Pointing with my finger, I carefully counted the following nineteen days that ended on a Sunday which had already been marked with a big red circle. Surely the whole world must know that it was finally my fourteenth birthday.

That day, I could just envision Mom and Dad coming into my room early in the morning (I would be pretending to be asleep), and saying, "Wake up, dear." And then, as they had so many times before, they would say, "Your time is coming." But this time it would be different. Instead of the words that stirred all sorts of troubled feelings inside—"But, it isn't here yet"—they would proclaim in unison: "Your time is coming, and it's finally here! You can go to the ward parties; you can go to the ward dances; you can go to the Christmas party, and you can even go with us to the social center to some of the stake dances." Could it be possible that I could live so long, another nineteen days?

The next couple of weeks moved slower than a snail's pace, and during that time Dad began talking about preparing the soil on our eighty acres and determining the proper time for planting. He considered the crops that would be most profitable according to the anticipated market and the readiness of the soil. But I had only one thought, and I wanted all the world to stand still and wait with me just a few more days. The rule was clear. At fourteen you could go to the dances. While for some teenagers in town such a statement meant *around* fourteen, I had learned that with children and crops Dad tried to eliminate any risk factors that might threaten a full harvest.

Was it possible that such ecstasy, so long anticipated, could ever be threatened? What could possibly happen now? These thoughts occurred to me as I heard the announcement in church about the big annual Relief Society party to be held on the anniversary of its organization—the seventeenth of March. Oh, why wasn't the Relief Society organized on the nineteenth or the twentieth or any date following? Could Dad and Mom possibly say no? Surely not if they loved me. That seemed evidence—they did love me, I felt quite sure. Could two days be that important? But I had to be sure.

At what seemed just the right time, I tried the positive approach and simply stated that "everyone" was going to the Relief Society party. From the delayed response I made a hopeful assumption. I have since learned that at that moment Dad was reaching for all the evidence he could grasp to support his position.

"Ardie," Dad said, "do you remember how much we pray for a long growing season on the farm, and how concerned we all are if it is cut short? Do you remember how we check the wheat daily in the fall until every kernel in every head of wheat has had time to mature before the harvest?"

Then coming to my chair and putting his arm around my shoulder while I stared at the table, tears streaming down my cheeks, he said in almost a pleading tone, "Can I be less concerned about my children?" And he waited. "It isn't the dance, my dear," he explained. "That wouldn't matter. It's much more than that." What more was there to his unreasonable logic, I thought, especially when he said he loved me? "It's the law of the harvest," he continued, "and there is a rule and a law. Having waited so long, would you break it for the sake of two days?" The question was left unanswered. The Relief

Society party came and went without me; and while my absence was not fatal, the possibility still seemed very likely, judging from the hurting I felt inside.

The memory of the many dances and parties which followed have since faded away with so many other youthful experiences, but the experience of that spring remains yet. When seeds are planted in the spring, a full season must pass before we can reap the harvest. And so it was that spring—the seeds of patience were planted and subjected to an imposed time line in hopes of ensuring a full harvest.

Seasons later, after many years and many springs, I again watch new life bursting forth in all living things—the little lambs, the calves, the trees, but above all in the greatest of all God's creations, his children. Here is the miracle of life in birth, in anxious anticipation of even yet another season. On occasion I hear my father's voice, not in the same words but clearly with the same message: "Your time is coming, my dear, but it isn't here yet." The familiarity of that message, that I had at one time resented so much, now in times of impatience and lack of understanding quiets my anxious heart.

"To every thing there is a season, and a time to every purpose under the heaven." (Ecclesiastes 3:1.)

Laundry Labels

I had no idea it would be like that. Had I only known, I'm sure my reaction would have been much different, but there was no way of knowing. The only missionaries who had ever visited our home were older men from the neighboring wards—stake missionaries, we called them.

Saturday afternoon Dad approached me with the request that I stay home from the dance that evening—the one event in my life that provided conversation for the rest of the week. Dad's request was not unreasonable, since Mom was in the hospital with pneumonia and the missionaries were coming for supper. But to miss a dance was like missing the roll call for life! And somehow hearing about the dance you missed always made it sound as if it had been the best one of the year.

"But, Dad," I said.

He interrupted to remind me that I didn't have to stay, I could suit myself. He then added, "But I would really appreciate it if you would help me out. Just fix supper and make the missionaries welcome."

What alternatives did I have? Anxious not to disappoint Dad (but even more anxious not to disappoint me), I grasped for what seemed like an acceptable solution.

"What about Grandma, Dad? Would it be all right if she would come? She could fix their supper and make them feel welcome."

"Yes, she could," was his reply, "but it wouldn't be the same."

Oh, why didn't he just say I couldn't go? Why did he say, "Suit yourself." How could I be mad at him when he left it up to me? Why did the missionaries have to stay in the bishop's home anyway? Why couldn't Dad delegate it to someone else, anyone else? But he didn't.

By six o'clock I was feeling like Joan of Arc—my great sacrifice in missing the dance was equal to being burned at the stake. With the attitude of a martyr, I set the table for our family plus additional places for the missionaries. I had no idea what these older brethren would enjoy eating, but decided on tomato soup and grilled cheese sandwiches—not fancy, but filling. With the last of the sandwiches prepared with cheese from our hometown cheese factory (in which we all took great pride) I heard a car drive into the yard. I walked to the window to see the cause of my weekend deprivation.

Could it be? I blinked my eyes once and then again. Dad hadn't told me. I didn't know. I wondered if he had known. The thoughts of missing the dance that had crowded my mind until I could think of nothing else suddenly dissipated. I hurried to the bathroom just off the kitchen and combed my hair, grateful that it still looked nice. Did I really look sixteen? I wondered. Maybe just a little older, I hoped.

Wanting to appear casual, I returned to the kitchen just as the missionaries came through the side door—six handsome knights in shining armor—courageous and bold, righteous and hungry. Dad, I thought, I'll always do what you want. Just ask anytime.

I didn't know if in all the history of our quiet little town any young missionaries had ever visited before, but today it seemed to me that history was being made before my very eyes. I knew the excitement would be recorded, if not in the annals of history, at least on the pages in my journal. It might read: "They were not older men; they were young men in dark suits, white shirts, and polished shoes, with nice smiles, warm handshakes . . . and. . . ."

I was so grateful that I had set the table with our nicest dishes even for the "older brethren." And the centerpiece of fresh flowers from our garden sort of blended in with the colors of the tablecloth, a thing I had not noticed before. Although I had somehow lost my appetite, everyone else seemed to enjoy his supper. During the meal Dad explained that the cheese was made in our hometown cheese factory which could be seen through the kitchen window. The consensus was that the sandwiches were delicious; and someone even said the tomato soup was good, which relieved me very much.

After supper, while I cleared the table and did the dishes, our guests sat around the table visiting with my family—all except one guest, that is. One of the missionaries helped me dry the dishes.

The following morning as part of our family stood on the porch waving good-bye, one of the missionaries, the same one who had helped dry the dishes, stopped before getting into the car to take a picture of us. I watched the car as it passed the cheese factory and continued on down the gravel road stirring the dust as it went.

What to others must have seemed like the conclusion of a nice experience was for me much more. My journal entry seemed of monumental importance and was recorded with great detail. Yet even that was not enough. In my heart I secretly yearned for some tangible evidence that this happening had actually occurred. In search of something that might serve that purpose, I hurried to the bedroom where two of the elders had slept. I surveyed the room quickly. Just as I had hoped, there in the wastebasket was the remaining proof— laundry labels from his shirt, the one who had helped me dry the dishes and had stopped to take a picture of our family. That they were from his shirt was verified by the location of the laundry printed on the labels, which corresponded to the field of labor where the elder was serving. In the privacy of the bedroom I rescued my evidence from the wastebasket. Folding the white printed labels carefully, I carried them to my bedroom and secretly tucked them away in the corner of the top drawer in my dresser.

Frequently, as evidence to my mind that the missionaries really had been there, I would get the labels out, unfold them, fold them again, and finally return them to the drawer. While those laundry labels were usually hidden from sight, the memory of the event they verified was never completely out of my mind.

As the weeks went by, even routine jobs became occasions for dreaming. Ironing Dad's white shirts now seemed less of a chore. I would stretch the collar to make it flat, and then iron it as perfectly as possible on both sides while thinking how it would be to iron a white shirt for that elder. The very thought gave wings to other dreams as my imagination provided the details. I thought of being in a Sunday School class with him there. The teacher would call on me for a scriptural reference and I would turn right to it while glancing out of the corner of my eye to see the look of admiration on the elder's face. And then there would be those special occasions when we might be discussing doctrine together (since at that time I thought that was all missionaries did), and I would casually quote various scriptures with the ease with which one might repeat the alphabet.

While I talked casually to my dad and mom about the missionaries and their visit, in my heart there was something much deeper. But who would understand? I thought. And then I began seriously talking to my Father in Heaven. Though my motives may have been in question, my desires were intense.

In my dreams I imagined that one day I would be in the position of discussing a particular passage in the Bible with that special missionary, and he would be surprised and impressed with my great knowledge of the scriptures. Even in my dreams I knew that such an experience was most unlikely, but I thought that perhaps I could increase the probability of such a thing ever happening if I were to begin now to do my part. The scriptures became more interesting to me as I would participate in an imaginary two-way conversation, asking the questions and giving what I thought were profound answers to passages I had just discovered.

One day as I was again ironing Dad's white shirts, a job which like magic had become a joyous chore, I considered the possibility of getting a letter through the mail with my name on the envelope and his signature inside. The thought of this possibility robbed my thoughts for a time, resulting in a heavy scorch mark in the shape of the iron right in the middle of the front of Dad's white shirt. That was hard to explain.

Three weeks later, like the replay of an event I had already experienced in my mind several times, I walked to the post office, took the mail from the postmaster, looked through the letters, and there it was! It really was. A small white envelope the size of a greeting card. It didn't exactly have my name on the front, but it did include me—*The Greene Family* it said. Nervously and quickly I tore open the envelope, which contained the most beautiful card I thought I had ever seen— small lavender violets clustered together around some fancy printing that read, "Thank You."

Standing in the middle of the road on my way back from the post office, I hugged the mail to me—all of it—then ran to the big tree by the house and sat on the lawn. Then I looked inside the card. There it was—a brief printed message expressing thanks, and below the message his signature—more evidence that my dreams were not all imaginary, as I had sometimes feared.

Out of the card fell a snapshot of our family standing on the front porch. Immediately my sense of appreciation was awakened, and I knew I must write back and thank him for the picture of our family. Somehow, Dad and Mom did not share the same urgent sense of social grace that I felt, but they did agree that since I had been the official hostess I could write a note (with the understanding that they would censor it for appropriateness) expressing thanks for the photo.

Mom thought I should wait at least a week before I mailed the letter I had written that very night. That gave me a chance to rewrite it several times, varying the stationery, the styles of writing, and the carefully selected words—which, incidentally, included a scripture from my growing resources. In addition to my expression of appreciation for the photo and the best wishes from the entire family, I casually indicated that I was preparing a two-and-a-half minute talk for the following Sunday. I thought this would surely be impressive to one spending his full time studying and teaching the gospel.

Time passed. It had been two months and two-and-a-half weeks since the day I mailed the letter from *The Greene Family*. I added to my secret treasure the thank-you card with the beautiful lavender violets on it. Each Monday, Wednesday, and Friday (mail days), and many times in between, I imagined the excitement of receiving a letter from him which would thank me for thanking him for the picture enclosed with the card that thanked us for our hospitality!

The regular dances in Cardston were still the highlight of our social activity for the year, and to miss even once was to threaten your social standing even more than the painful experience of being left standing alone waiting to be asked to dance after almost everyone else was on the floor. (While that dreadful experience didn't happen often, the possibility that it might was of genuine concern to all of the girls. My friends and I used to practice smiling in the way we would try to if one of us were the only one left without a partner. It was very difficult, even with practice.)

By late fall I discovered that my own two-way conversation with the scriptures was improving, and furthermore my secret motives had prompted other interests. My cooking skills were increasing beyond tomato soup and grilled cheese sandwiches. Sometimes I would look through the cookbook and imagine that the missionaries might be coming for supper again. On those occasions the family frequently benefited from my self-imposed social responsibilities.

In early spring we were advised that there would be another missionary conference in Cardston about mid-June, and the missionaries would need accommodations at the bishops' or other members' homes in the neighboring wards. No explanation was needed for my willingness (even eagerness) to help in preparing for our family responsibility. While I didn't know if the same missionaries would be assigned to our home, even the possibility that it could happen made all the preparation worthwhile. Without encouragement from Mom I began the housecleaning early that spring. Even the corners in the back bedrooms got special attention as I imagined how a representative from *Good Housekeeping* (looking very much like that special elder), would marvel at the thoroughness of my cleaning skills.

With the earnestness of my preparation the days flew by, and suddenly it was June and time for the conference. While I knew Dad had no responsibility for the assignment of the missionaries who were to be guests in our home, I felt quite sure that our Father in Heaven did, and so I talked with him about it. But as I had learned from previous experiences, prayers aren't always answered just the way we hope at the time, and what we think is a no to a fervent prayer might really be a yes to an even higher request.

The missionaries who stayed with us were nice, and I was glad the house was clean, but it was attending the mission conference with my parents that became the all-consuming thought now. Would he be there? And if he were there, would he remember me? And if he did, would he shake hands? And if he did. . . ?

We arrived early. Many members and missionaries were mingling together in the foyer. My heart was pounding as we made our way into the chapel a few minutes early and took our seats near the front. It was announced from the pulpit that the district presidents should take their places on the stand. I watched them come up the aisle as best I could without turning my head, my eyes straining to extend my peripheral vision. I saw him out of the corner of my eye in real life. He was sitting in front of me now but I dared not look up, not until I got my composure which took a minute. Finally I looked at him, and he smiled. I smiled back. Then I looked at Dad. He was also smiling as he nodded. Then I wasn't sure who the elder was smiling at, me or Dad!

It was a special meeting. I was excited and surprised when I realized how many of the scriptures I knew about missionary work that were being quoted.

Following the meeting, I watched the elder leave the stand and come toward us. He shook hands with Dad, was introduced to my mom, and then shook hands with me. It seemed that maybe he held my hand a little longer, or was it tighter? In our conversation he inquired about my brother, who was away at school, and my younger sisters. Dad responded to his questions graciously, then he asked me about my plans for school and where I intended to go to college. I mentioned Brigham Young University, and I thought I heard him say, "Maybe I'll see you there someday." Mom and Dad didn't remember hearing that part.

Driving home in the car, I reviewed that brief conversation over and over and over again in my mind. I was sure I had heard him say maybe he would see me there someday. And then I wondered—was the maybe dependent upon my being there or upon his? And if we were both there, what did "maybe I'll see you there" mean?

During the next two years I made many important entries in my journal. There were special friends, special occasions, good times, and challenging times. I soon discovered that having a definite goal in mind affected my choices, my priorities, and, in fact, everything I did as I dreamed of attending BYU.

With a multitude of happenings between that first

missionary conference and my enrollment at the university, I had learned that some dreams when converted to goals can become a reality. The preparation that had finally brought me to BYU was being rewarded. While I left the laundry labels at home in my drawer, I brought with me the rewards of their motivation. I had learned to cook, to clean, and to study. But, perhaps even more important, I had experienced the great joy of reaching one goal as I stood on the threshold of another. Gradually I had developed increased confidence as I served with others in response to many calls from Church leaders. I discovered the growth and blessings that come from service. Even if that special elder didn't see me at the Y (although I still hoped he would), I was excited about all the possibilities to choose from, decisions to make, new goals to set and reach, and mountains to climb.

It was the spring of the year, April, and time for General Conference. The flowers on Temple Square were more beautiful than I had ever seen them before; and contrary to tradition, there was no snow or rain—just sunshine and blue skies. That special elder had returned home from his mission. He had invited me to attend the conference with him in the Tabernacle. We sat in the balcony on the north side. I wondered in my heart about this historic building. Could other historic events have their beginning here?

The prophet spoke. We listened together. The speakers awakened within me an increased desire to set new goals and to reach higher, as they stressed the need for greater dedication and commitment.

On the way home we talked a lot about the conference. It was exciting to discover that he shared the same feelings I had and many of the same goals. I liked what he thought, and he said he liked what I thought.

Now, years and years later, having ironed Elder Kapp's white shirts for over a quarter of a century, I think again of the laundry labels still tucked away with my treasures. I think of laundry labels and impossible dreams that with preparation become realities.

The Call Home

The car rolled completely over. Somehow, we were upright again but off the road and headed in the opposite direction. The silence was deafening. I could feel my heart pounding against my chest, and my shoulder was hurting just a little.

My brother, Kay, who had been driving, pushed the door open on his side, got out, and walked around Dad's new car. After examining the mashed-in door on one side, the caved-in top, and the broken headlights, he sat again in the driver's seat and then broke the silence. In a tone of deep remorse he groaned,"Oh-h-h, no!" As he held his head in his hands, I shared his feelings of hopelessness.

When we had left our home about an hour before, we knew that Mom and Dad were anxious about our safety on the icy, wintry roads. But Kay and I had insisted that this basketball game in a neighboring town was one we couldn't miss. We had persisted. The roads were bad, but it wasn't really cold—just a little below freezing; and besides Dad himself had often said that Kay was just as good a driver as he was.

Before we left, Dad had expressed his concern again, reminding us of the dangers of the frozen ruts even when driving at a reasonable speed. "You know you can lose control completely if the car begins to slide on the frozen ground," he warned. We already knew that, since we ourselves had lived through what seemed to us quite a few winters and had gained some experience at driving on these treacherous roads. But if you never left home when the roads were bad, you might as well be in hibernation through the long, long winters and miss at least half of the experiences in life, we reasoned. Mom instructed us to hurry home, then added, "But don't drive too fast." We promised to be careful and quickly got ready to go.

Three of our friends went with us. We left in plenty of time to allow for the poor road conditions. My brother drove very carefully, with no "nonsensing around."

At the ten-mile turnoff we headed north across the reservation. Dad was right. The roads truly were bad. The ruts he had warned us about were very real—and deeper than I remembered.

We proceeded cautiously, but in spite of our good intentions somehow the car began to slide. Kay quickly turned the wheel; the car would not respond. The use of the brake was never an alternative on icy roads, so he just kept working with the wheel. But the car was slipping further and further sideways and picking up speed.

Bump! Bump! Bump! We were thrown against each other as the car rolled—first hitting the passenger side, then the top, and then landing on the wheels again.

After Kay finally broke the silence, we began sharing our feelings—what we thought had happened, how we felt physically, what Dad and Mom would say, and what we should do. One thing we knew for sure—we were sorry, really sorry. We knew how much Dad and Mom loved this car and how long they had saved for it. I thought of our persistence even when they didn't want us to go, and wished we could go through all that again. But this time I would do it differently. I wouldn't be so insistent. No one had been hurt in the accident, but inside I felt awful.

Only moments later a car stopped to offer help. Inside were

some of our friends who were on their way to the same game. We told them what had happened, and they offered to take us with them and to bring us home afterwards. (I wished we were going home with them right then.) They didn't seem to mind being crowded, and we were very grateful.

When we had reached our destination, we immediately found a telephone so we could call home. I had agreed to give the accounting of our frightening experience. It's hard to call home when you're in trouble, yet I said a prayer in my heart that Dad and Mom would be there.

I reached the Glenwood operator and asked for our number, number three. Luckily, we had twenty-four-hour telephone service these days. The operator rang the number, but there was no answer. My hands began to tremble. She immediately came on the line explaining that my folks were at a neighbor's house visiting, and she would ring them there. The operators in our little village had a way of keeping track of everyone—if the person you wanted to talk with was in town, he could be located.

By now my heart was pounding harder and I could feel myself shaking all over, especially my legs. It seemed as if my knees didn't want to hold me up. I wanted to cry. I wished I were home. As soon as I heard Dad's voice, I began to cry.

"Dad," was all I could say through my sobbing.

"Are you okay? Are you okay?" he repeated, with great concern.

"Yes, Dad," I cried. "We're okay." I heard his heavy sigh of relief. "But Dad," I choked, "your new car—it's all mashed." And then I told him how Kay had lost control and what had happened.

"My dear," he said, "don't you worry about that car." I could tell by the tone of his voice that he loved us a thousand times more than he did his new car.

He inquired again about each one of us, making sure that no one was hurt, then talked about arranging to come and get us. I explained that we had a way home after the game. He asked again if each of us was okay, then said, "I'll worry about the car tomorrow, but tonight I'll just give thanks for your safety."

When we arrived home that night, Dad and Mom were waiting up for us. We felt their love and reassurance which we needed so much at that time. That experience did not limit our use of the car after Dad got it repaired. He said that such a thing could have happened to him, but that we must try always to be prepared for the unpredictable problems that can occur in winter travel. And then he reminded us, as he often had, "Be sure to call home if you're going to be late or if you're ever in trouble."

Some years later, having returned home from college for the Christmas holidays, I again faced the hazards of winter travel. According to tradition in our area, all the young people (whether home from school or living at home) within a radius of about thirty-five miles gathered at the social center in Cardston for a Christmas dance. There the warmth of renewed friendships, a good dance band, elaborate decorations, and plentiful refreshments diminished the thought of the cold temperatures outdoors, but not so much that we failed to take every precaution to ensure our safe return home.

It had been the perfect social that night, worth driving all the way to Canada for, I thought. It seemed as if everyone was there. My dance card was filled almost immediately and, except that the evening went so fast, the whole occasion was just perfect.

About thirty minutes before the dance was over, my date went out in the forty-degree-below-zero weather to warm up the motor of the car. This was absolutely necessary to keep the radiator from freezing in the extremely cold temperatures.

With the strains of the last waltz still ringing in our ears, we reluctantly left the dance. The dry, thin snow crunched under our feet and the cold air stung our nostrils as we ran to the car. But the warmth of friendship would sustain us on the cold ride home.

The Indian reservation lay between our town and Cardston. There were very few houses sprinkled across this vast area—no other buildings, no trees, nothing to break the harsh wind that swept across the road against the snow fences, carving cavities in the high drifts.

About three miles out, we spotted a car along the side of the road. The danger to life and limb on a night such as this would never allow anyone to consider passing someone up, not anyone. We couldn't see very clearly through the heavily crusted frost that coated the windows of their car, but its occupants looked familiar to us. Without wasting time for talk, two couples who turned out to be our friends, crowded into our car. To open the door long enough for them to get in was to sacrifice considerable warmth, so precious on a night like this.

Their gas line had frozen up. It was decided that we should turn around and go back to Cardston. If a garage was still open, we could get something that would thaw the gas line and take care of that problem.

Before leaving town the second time, I went into the garage and called home. Mom answered and then called Dad. I explained the details of our plight but assured him that everything was going to be all right. But just in case of trouble, we checked our watches and determined about what time we should arrive home. If we were not on schedule, he should come to our rescue.

Again we started out across the reservation. The wind chill continued to lower the temperature. We reached our friends' car, but their efforts to start it were in vain and continued attempts only increased the danger to all of us. Without any discussion we crowded together in one car, grateful for the added warmth of so many bodies, and headed for home.

Only a few miles further into the blizzard we discovered that no heat was coming from our car—we were frozen up. We came to a slow stop. By now, the memory of the dance had faded somewhat and the conversation was free of any unnecessary chatter. While we watched the snow swirling in front of the windshield, we listened to each other's suggestions as to what we might do. The side windows were already frozen over. Yet we felt a great sense of relief, there in the quiet of the car, when I reminded everyone that I had called home.

After several minutes an old truck pulled alongside us. We rolled down our window just a crack, and they did the same. Hearing of our plight, these Indians—our rescuers—got a chain from the back of their truck, hooked it to our bumper, and agreed to pull us as far as the turnoff.

They had included alcohol in their celebration of the holidays, so the ride to the turnoff became a wild experience. Our speed only added to our anxious concern. We would get there in a hurry—provided we got there at all.

At the turnoff they unhooked their chain from our car, and we thanked them most sincerely. As they drove out of sight, the threat of the cold again weighed on us. We waited.

"How long do you think it will be before your Dad will get here?" questioned someone in the back seat.

"Well," I explained, "if he waits until the time we should have been home before he leaves, we'll have to wait at least another half hour."

While no one complained, we all felt that it would be a long half hour, even huddled together under the two blankets we always carried during winter travel. With our fingernails we tried to scrape a small opening in the frost-coated windows so we could watch for any sign of car lights coming from the west.

I kept thinking how glad I was that I had called home, and yet I knew that even without the call, if we were later than we were expected to be, Dad would be out after us. I knew we could depend on that. I remembered the time some years before when Dad had come after me because it was late. But that time it was a summer party, and I didn't need him. In fact, I was so embarrassed I thought I would die. Tonight, I knew that his coming would allow us to live. Reports of people freezing to death while stranded along the country roads at this time of year were not infrequent.

"Your dad is coming!" someone shouted. "I can see his lights!"

We were sure no one else would be coming in this direction on a night like this. I realized that Dad had not waited to come to our rescue. He must have left home right after my call, waiting only long enough to warm up his car before taking off across the reservation. There was no yellow line to follow on the side road he traveled, but then Dad knew that road like the back of his hand and was well acquainted with all the hazards. As the lights drew closer we began singing, "For he's a jolly, good fellow," assured now that our safety and comfort were only minutes away.

A man got out of his car, his bulky parka almost obscuring his face, but there was no question that it was my dad. Who else would respond so quickly in time of need? We all piled into his car, even more crowded now with nine people, and safely returned home.

Later, I thought about what might have happened if the telephone lines had been down, as they sometimes were during severe winter storms, but then I realized that Dad would have been there when we needed him anyway. He always knew where we were and when we should be home, and he came after us if we weren't there.

I remembered his looking for my sister one night after a dance when she should have been in. He went to see if she was in need of help (whether she thought she needed it or not). Finally, he returned without her but with considerable concern. Mom met him at the door, anxious to explain that Sharon had come home from the dance early, before Mom and Dad arrived home. Since no one was home, she had gone to bed. After that, Dad always made his first investigation at home.

Winter travel always presented some risks, but unless you planned to stay indoors six months out of the year you prepared as best you could and tried to carry on life as usual. That was the situation the winter my husband and I came home for Christmas. He had had considerable experience in these extreme temperatures, and the dangers seemed less of a concern than the disappointment he knew I would feel from not being with my family for our traditional Christmas.

The weather seemed in our favor this year, and we had made our way northward through snowy mountain passes and then out across the prairie to our destination without mishap. Christmas had turned out to be perfect in every way—the parties, the dances, the shared family traditions, good food, games, and the huge jigsaw puzzle that was an annual project to fit together in the moments when something else wasn't going on.

The days slipped by quickly. Now, holding a big lunch of turkey sandwiches, oranges, apples, and Christmas cake, and taking two extra blankets and a shovel with us, we bade everyone good-bye again, then climbed into our car to begin the seven-hundred-mile trip home.

The weather forecast had not been good, but commitments at home and at work forced us to leave. Another couple, (friends of ours), was traveling with us; they also carried a big lunch and an extra blanket.

We had been driving for about an hour when a heavy storm began closing in. We watched anxiously, not sharing our growing concerns with each other. Big snowflakes swirling in the car lights soon had a hypnotic effect. We kept blinking and straining to see the yellow line that appeared only now and again down the center of the highway. If we could just reach the border crossing between Canada and the United States, we were sure we could make it to a nearby town and get a motel for the night. It was the only reasonable thing to do. A silence came over us.

At the border we were advised that it was forty-two degrees below zero, the winds were increasing in velocity, and we should not continue on. We readily agreed with that suggestion and determined to stay overnight in Shelby.

The blizzard obscured even the lights from the commercial

buildings, but we located a motel and went in. The lobby was crowded with people. "No rooms," was the response to our inquiry. "No rooms anywhere in town. We've checked every available facility and everything is full," said the man at the counter. We squeezed our way single file back through the smoke and noise and the anxious people expressing their frustrations.

Once more in the car, thoughtful and concerned, we took stock of our situation. We would have to stay in the car all night, and we would need to keep the engine running to keep warm. It was agreed that we might as well continue on to the next town sixty miles away.

The roads were not snowpacked, actually they were clear. But the fierce wind, while scouring the road, carried with it the blinding snow. We drove very slowly as we strained our eyes watching for the yellow line. After about forty minutes we became disoriented, dizzy, and unsure about distance or direction. We stopped to change drivers. My friend's husband had agreed to take a turn. At least we would keep moving. We traveled only about one block when the blinding snow completely obscured his vision, causing him to drive off the road. Our efforts to get back on were of no avail. Our anxiety rose.

My husband, Heber, got out to survey the situation and came back, his eyebrows and eyelashes frozen. He reported that one back tire was on the asphalt and other only six inches away. He thought that with the bumper jack he could raise the car and then push it over far enough to get both tires onto the highway.

We wrapped scarves around his head and over his face, leaving just an opening for his eyes before he went out again. Waiting anxiously, we could hear the sequence of his efforts. The trunk of the car being opened; the left rear wheel being raised. Then nothing. We waited.

Heber got back in the car and explained that the jack had locked. He couldn't get it up or down. There were no alternatives. Again he tried in vain to back up onto the road. With his hands on the steering wheel, I noticed white frozen spots on his wrists between his gloves and overcoat. He tried to back up once again. This time the engine killed. He tried to start the engine. It wouldn't start.

We looked at each other, hardly breathing. Without heat the metal body of a car turns into an icebox almost immediately in such extreme temperatures. Would this be our entombment—out here where there were no lights, no buildings, no telephone lines, and no help? No, it would not. The power lines were not down; we knew we could call home. Together we bowed our heads in prayer. Each, in turn, spoke aloud to our Father in Heaven and told him of our desperate plight.

When the last prayer had been offered, Heber said he felt impressed, even at the risk of opening the door again, to lift the hood of the car and see what he might find. For the first time he observed that the starter in this particular car could be turned by hand. He instructed me to pump the gas when I heard the engine start. Gripping the steering wheel and holding my foot ready on the gas pedal, I strained to hear any sound that might come from the engine. I repeated a silent prayer, "Father, let us get heat in this car somehow."

The engine coughed once—then again. I pumped the gas quickly at first, then held it steady. My breathing became more steady also. The car engine turned over—the engine was running. We would have heat. Heber got back into the car. We knew the source of our lifesaving blessing, but we were not out of danger yet. It would be hours before morning, and we were still in need of help. Again, we supplicated the Lord; and then waited.

By now I was feeling very weary and very cold. I had read that the process of freezing to death begins with feeling drowsy—eventually you just fall asleep, and you never wake up. We were all sleepy, and I was scared.

I remembered again the time when we were so much in need

of help and Dad had met us at the turnoff. I didn't know just how it would be this time, but we had called home in prayer and I felt that somehow help would come.

About twenty minutes passed, according to our watches, and we sat almost in silence. The fierce wind howling around us continued to buffet the car. We had cleared a little spot in the thick frost on the back window. Suddenly, my friend said she thought she saw a light coming toward us. Her husband quickly verified what she saw. It was no illusion. Help was coming. We hugged each other.

We could see more clearly now. It was a big semitrailer with lights all over it. It looked more beautiful to me than the Christmas tree in our living room. The truck drove up beside us and stopped. Rolling down his window, the driver shouted at us. He got down from his cab, came to our car, and continued shouting, adding swear words to give emphasis to his questions.

"What the _ _ _ _ are you doing out on a night like this? Don't you know better? Don't you have better sense?" He then continued his chastisement to include himself. "I don't know why I'm out on a night like this. I know better!"

In spite of his anger he was concerned about us and anxious to help. Yes, even to save our lives. He pulled our car back onto the road and instructed us to follow his taillights. He would guide us into town.

Following the lights on his truck that shone through the storm, we found the swirling snow less blinding. We concentrated on the red taillights and tried to forget the storm. Once into town the trucker drove by a motel, honked while rolling his window down, then waved to us and drove on. We watched the lifesaving light disappear again into the storm.

"God does notice us, and he watches over us. But it is usually through another person that he meets our needs." (Spencer W. Kimball, "Small Acts of Service," *Ensign*, December 1974, page 5.)

The
School Bell

There are times in my life, moments of exultation, when I find the world so inexpressibly beautiful, when everything holds such meaning that my soul reaches out with yearning for eager indulgence and would, if possible, consume too much too fast. But nature usually holds control over the hurried passerby and reveals in measured amounts, only after exacting the price of pausing, an experience for which there are no words.

At those times, not often, but recurring frequently enough to live in quiet anticipation, the soul seems to beat in rhythm with the pulse of the earth; and echoes return again and again like the theme of a great symphony, not void of the pain and suffering which is a part of this world but returning in a larger context where an eternal balance makes all things beautiful. After our family moved away, we went back to our prairie again and again over the years to awaken echoes, however faint, of those moments of exultation—the fragrant smell of the damp earth after a spring rain, the concert of night sounds after sundown, and the faintly audible croaking of frogs as similar sounds in the distance respond in steady rhythm.

We were all aware that this would be the last time we would return to our prairie together. In the early morning as the sun began edging its way across the big prairie sky, Dad raised up from his sickbed in the car to make an almost reverent yet fervent declaration to each of us, based on years of well-grounded experiences: "This prairie has never looked more beautiful. It's at its very best for my last inspection." Though our eyes were blurred with tears, they were opened to a vision that magnified any previous insights.

On that morning of reverence, as we drove along the prairie highway that disappeared over the distant horizon, the echoes of the past came flooding back, layer upon layer, like the bands of color spreading out on either side from the yellow ribbon that divided the newly paved road on which we traveled. At the edge of the blacktop, which appeared to be freshly washed by the morning dew, was a border of exquisite wild flowers tucked in among the tall grasses that helped fill the borrow pit. The flowers spread across to the fence line and blended into the next layer of color.

Across the fences the green patches of grain alternating with bright yellow fields of maize and a few cultivated clearings seemed to crowd toward the base of the gray-blue foothills in the distance. This varied band of color appeared to be never-ending until it joined the deeper purple mountains and reached upward to the blue sky resting fragilely against the peaks of the rugged Canadian Rockies. The feathery clouds caught the morning sun, casting a pinkish glow over all, as if to announce a divine blessing on this sacred experience.

After we turned off the main road past Bullhorn Cooley and drove through the river bottom toward "our stomping" grounds," as Dad called it, we came upon our quiet little village in all its prairie splendor. Thoughts came crowding into my mind. *Does honeysuckle really have honey in it? Do the tips of alsike clover when pulled from their pincushionlike base really taste sweet when you put them to your lips and sip? Do the wild roses ever smell as sweet as I remembered, and does*

94

soaking their leaves in a jar of water really make rose-scented perfume?

We stopped the car near the edge of town (which wasn't too far from the other edge of town) and began our experience in rediscovery. We came upon the mound of a root cellar covered by a tangled wild rose bush and a large clump of sweet clover that we had forgotten. We saw the two big trees on either side of the gate leading to a path now grown over by grass and weeds. Occasionally we discovered things that had always been there, but we hadn't remembered seeing them before because they were so completely commonplace; but more often we saw in our mind's eye the vividness of things that were no longer there, but which remained indelibly imprinted upon our senses.

We sauntered haltingly down the gravel road past the tall cottonwood trees on the south side of the now vacant lot where the old school had been. For us the school still remained and with that memory came a chain of reflections like dominoes tumbling one after another.

Dad took the lead. "It was the old bell," he said, and we all looked in the same direction, seeing it clearly in our mind's eye. "The school bell kept us in line," he continued. "It was the bell that kept us moving." And then, as if carried away to days long since gone, he explained: "Brother Savage, an old Englishman, was always meticulous about keeping accurate time. He never varied. There were two bells," Dad went on, "a fifteen-minute bell would ring six times, giving ample warning before the final five-minute bell sounded a simple dingdong—and you'd better be there." His weakened voice increased in intensity as he added, "It's important to listen for the bell."

My sister Sharon recalled for us the recess bell that called the students into position, side by side, boys on one side and girls on the other. Each right hand was brought to rest on the shoulder of the student in front to ensure good, straight lines symbolic of the uncompromising regulations which increased our ready response to the sound of the bell and which reminded

us to be where we were supposed to be. We all agreed that, for a time at least, the old bell had played a major part in each of our lives and, though it had been silenced for years, the effects of its clear and dependable ringing, like reverberating sound waves, were still deep within each of us, prompting the same regularity and dependability.

As we mused together in silence for a time I pondered the possibility of my own inner bell being silenced, if only for a moment, just a rest break, maybe. As if reading my thoughts, Dad lay back on the soft, grassy ditch bank where we had stopped and began with a familiar phrase we had all learned to love. "I remember a story in the old fourth-grade reader," he said. I often wondered why it was always the fourth-grade reader he quoted, but nevertheless I was eager to hear another one of his stories from that source which I had come to believe had no limits.

He began to tell his story, and we all leaned forward to catch every word just as we always had. "There was an old and very large Inchcape Rock," he began. "It got its name from being located just one inch below the water's surface where it couldn't be seen, and it lay dangerously in the path of the mariners returning from sea. Many seamen had lost their ships and their lives because of the rock, especially in times of storm."

By now we were eager to learn what this had to do with the school bell, and Dad continued. "There was an abbot in the small seashore town of Aberbrothok who devised a solution to this life-threatening hazard. With great care and in the face of considerable danger, the abbot fastened a buoy with a large bell on it to the Inchcape Rock. From then on the bell rang continuously and faithfully with the motion of the waves of the sea."

Over the years Dad had developed a style of storytelling that often made the pauses the greatest moments for learning. He waited for us to envision the details, then went on. "When the mariners would come within hearing distance of the bell on

Inchcape Rock"—his explanation broke into a rhyme—"they would bless the Abbot of Aberbrothok."

"Ralph, the Rover, was a bit of a pirate, and he disliked the abbot and disliked even more the praises the abbot received from the mariners whose lives he'd spared. So one day Ralph, the Rover, cut the bell from the Inchcape Rock." And the rhyme continued:

> Down sank the Bell with a gurgling sound;
> The bubbles rose, and burst around.
> Quoth Sir Ralph, "The next who comes to the Rock
> Won't bless the Abbot of Aberbrothok."
>
> Sir Ralph, the Rover, sailed away,
> He scoured the seas for many a day.

More narrative followed. "On his way back it was night and the sea was high, and he thought the moon would be up. And in the darkness he said with great anxiety (but only to himself), 'I wish I could hear the bell of the Inchcape Rock.' "

> Sir Ralph, the Rover, tore his hair;
> He cursed himself in his despair.
> The waves rush in on every side;
> The ship is sinking beneath the tide.
> (Robert Southey, "The Inchcape Rock.")

As always, Dad's story stood without editorializing, left for the mind of those so choosing to explore its meaning. I thought again of the inner bell, but this time rather than wishing to silence its constant peal, I felt myself strain a little that I might hear it more clearly.

We interrupted our rediscovery for a time so that Dad could have rest for his body—but his thoughts continued to feed us. At times those thoughts seemed unrelated; it was left to each of us to pick them up, string them on a common thread, and then see them in relationship, as jewels of eternal worth.

After our morning adventure, Dad stretched out on the couch in the home where we had arranged to stay for a few days. Without introduction, as if time for teaching might be running short, he quoted, "For if the trumpet give an uncertain sound, who shall prepare himself to battle?" (1 Corinthians 14:8.)

At that moment I recalled a gift presented to me by my father months before—a small, beautifully cut crystal bell. Adding this to the scripture and the common thread of thought, I wondered if there was a message originally intended that I had only now discovered. Yes, there was, I decided; and I wondered about other lessons yet to be discovered.

On the morning that we said our farewells to dear friends, looked once more at precious surroundings, and then headed eastward down the paved highway which had replaced the dusty, old gravel road we remembered so well, I sensed the apex of this sacred happening. "I'm ready to go home now," Dad said, looking straight ahead as far as the eye could see, out to where the sky came down to meet the horizon as the sun was just rising in all its prairie splendor.

I found myself attentive, listening, wanting to share something of this moment of sweet hurting; and from deep inside, a distant sound like a divine echo could be heard ringing. A bell, I thought. Maybe the fifteen-minute bell to prepare us so that we might each be in our place when the day begins.

A Bridge for Crossing

It was early morning as I stood alone on the bridge near my home witnessing the dawning of a new day. The signs of winter were slipping away, and the warm rays of the sun permitted only the peaks of the mountains to retain their wintery snows. Standing on the edge of the bridge with my fingers through the chain-link fence, I could see a few tender green shoots forcing their way through the earthy floor below. The water in the creek was bubbling over an old log and around some big rocks near the bank—just as it had last fall. The tall pine trees bordered the creek on both sides, steadfast in their silent vigil.

Staring at the stream continually flowing past a given point in the freshness of the new day left me transfixed for a time. It was as if the same water that I had watched just a season ago had been recycled. There appeared to be no difference in the scene, except that this time Dad was not with me. Last fall, when we stood together with our fingers through the chain-link fence gazing at the water below, he had told me it would be like this.

A Bridge for Crossing

The bridge had been under construction for over a year, and each day Dad had watched the gradual erection of this concrete structure that would eventually span the gully over the boulevard and allow us to cross. Dad's walks always included this daily inspection of the bridge before he made his way back up the hill to our home. Then he would report on the progress being made. Sometimes his concern for the days when no workers showed up on the job gave the impression that there might have been a schedule for completion for which he was to be held accountable. He had carefully followed the pouring of the footings, then the rising of the concrete piers, the addition of the steel reinforcement, and for some time now the deliberate movements of a huge crane with its giant jaws open to the sky.

One evening in the twilight, the noise of construction for that day quieted, Dad and I stood leaning against a big earth-moving tractor at the bridge site. No traffic interrupted our privacy, since there was as yet no bridge for crossing.

"Dad," I asked in a teasing tone, "how come you're so anxious about the completion of this bridge?"

He smiled, stroked his chin, and without any introduction or explanation began quoting from his reservoir of memorized poetry:

> An old man, going a lone highway,
> Came at the evening, cold and gray,
> To a chasm, vast and deep and wide,
> Through which was flowing a sullen tide.
> The old man crossed in the twilight dim;
> The sullen stream had no fears for him;
> But he turned when safe on the other side
> And built a bridge to span the tide.
>
> "Old man," said a fellow pilgrim near,
> "You are wasting strength with building here;
> Your journey will end with the ending day;
> You never again will pass this way;

You have crossed the chasm, deep and wide—
Why build you the bridge at eventide?"

The builder lifted his old gray head:
"Good friend, in the path I have come," he said,
"There followeth after me today
A youth whose feet must pass this way.
This chasm that has been naught to me
To that fair-haired youth may a pitfall be.
He, too, must cross in the twilight dim;
Good friend, I am building the bridge for him."

>   (Will Allen Dromgoole, "The Bridge Build-
>   er," *Golden Nuggets of Thought,* comp. Ezra
>   L. Marler, 4 vols. [Salt Lake City: Bookcraft,
>   Inc., 1946-63], 1:18-19.)

I don't know how long I stood alone gazing at the water in the creek below, reliving those scenes and sounds of the previous fall. Letting go of my grip on the fence, I slowly straightened my fingers one by one. Like the flow of the water, my thoughts could not be stopped.

"Carcinoma," the doctor explained. "The entire stomach is filled with cancer and must be removed." *But why my dad?* I thought. *He has been in such good health,* I reasoned, *and lived such a good life, and my mom needs him; and I need him; we all need him.*

On that afternoon our father gathered us together and gave us the sobering report himself in every detail as he understood it. Then, very much aware of our anxious concern and over the years having become a master of the teaching moment, he asked each of us to get our scriptures. Sitting next to Mom, he told us to turn to Alma 40:11-12, then began reading from his well-worn scriptures while we each followed along in ours:

> Now, concerning the state of the soul between death and the resurrection—Behold, it has been made known unto me by an angel, that the spirits of all men, as soon as they are departed from this mortal body, yea the spirits of all men, whether they be good or evil, are taken home to that God who gave them life.
>
> And then shall it come to pass, that the spirits of those who are righteous are received into a state of happiness, which is called paradise, a state of rest, a state of peace, where they shall rest from all their troubles and from all care, and sorrow.

Those familiar words now carried a different message than ever before.

Following the surgery, we brought Dad home from the hospital—thin and weak in body but undaunted in spirit. It had been raining gently all day. In the evening, after a much-needed rest, Dad insisted on going for a little walk. We put our coats on and walked around the house to the brow of the hill. From there we could see the tall crane down by the bridge. We looked over the garden area below. We savored a drenched and dripping apple tree close by, millions of silver droplets adorning its deep green leaves. We smelled the fragrance of the rain-soaked earth.

For a time we stood in silence. The rain fell gently, tapping on the umbrella. Then the feelings we could no longer contain began spilling out. Dad talked about the sweetness and sacredness of these times and spoke of the nearness of the Lord. He told me that to deny the hurting feelings inside would be to deny the precious memories from which they sprang. "And like birth pains," he said, "they can open a passageway to new understanding." Tears, like drops of rain, fell from my chin to the damp earth at my feet. Like a cleansing, the hurt was washed away for the moment, and we returned to the house.

According to Dad's wishes, as a family we had returned to

Canada in midsummer "for one last inspection of the old stomping grounds." Following that visit, one after another the days brought visible evidence that the progression of his spirit was rapidly outgrowing his physical body. The process was so natural, like a cocoon giving way to release a butterfly for extended flight.

Each member of the family, now, as in days past, had special times with Dad. His daily walk to the bridge, now nearing completion, was my time. He needed my assistance to get back up the hill, and I needed his strength to help me climb the steep slope ahead. I had often wondered what people talked about when they had to face a "final graduation," as Dad called it. I found myself anxiously awaiting each new insight that began to unfold as my gifted teacher seemed to plan the lesson for each day. Knowing that I was anticipating a release from an important assignment, he personalized his instruction for me. "All I hope for is an honorable release. That's really all one could ask," Dad said. Then with a faint smile he slipped his arm around my waist. "We can give each other an honorable release—but we'll never be released from each other." With my arm around him to support his frail body, we came back up the hill.

It was a Wednesday morning. Dad had gone down to the garden to check on his strawberry plants. He said that with the help of his cane he was sure he could make it. About an hour later the doorbell rang and there stood a neighbor, a former Canadian, with her hands behind her back and a mischievous look on her face. Without any comment she quickly brought both hands in front of her and presented me with a giant bouquet of yellow wild flowers. "Buffalo beans!" I exclaimed. "Wherever did you get them?"

Excited with her surprise for me, she said: "I haven't seen buffalo beans since I left the ditch banks of Alberta. I wanted to share them with you because I knew you'd be excited to have some too." After thanking her, with both hands I reached out not only for the buffalo beans but for all the memories that came flooding back with them.

104

Moments later I ran down the garden path with my hands behind my back. Dad was sitting on the ground tending his strawberry plants. Looking up, he smiled—his face thin, his eyes bright. I felt like a child reliving an incident long past. Kneeling beside him on the ground with my hands still behind my back, I quickly thrust my treasure in front of him. His eyes grew big. "Buffalo beans!" he exclaimed. And then again in a more reverent tone, "buffalo beans." He reached for them and breathed deeply as he buried his face in those glorious blossoms.

As if part of an instant replay triggered by the wild flowers, we were once more sitting together on the ditch banks of our farm and reliving the precious memories of those days now past.

Having lost all track of time, Dad brought us abruptly back to the present when he asked, "Do you think there'll be buffalo beans over there?" We both agreed unquestionably. Those tiny pillow-like blossoms, like puffs of sunshine clustered together, would adorn the ditch banks over there. Along the narrow path enclosed like a tunnel in the oak brush I slowly followed Dad back up the hill from the garden. By taking frequent rests, we finally made it to the top. As we came out into the clearing near the house I again put my arm around his thin waist to assist him. 'I'll miss you when I go," he said. I swallowed hard, but could not answer.

While Mom and Dad sat together tenderly holding hands like young sweethearts, I went upstairs to the kitchen to place our treasured flowers in water. Leaning over to smell them just once more, I again recalled with vividness all that Dad and I had shared that morning. On my knees, my arms resting on the counter top, for a multitude of precious memories relived I could only bow my head and sum up my feelings of gratitude in a simple prayer: "Father, thank you for the buffalo beans and for Sister Van Orman who brought them to us."

Late in the afternoon on another day Dad and I headed for the bridge. Our arms were now laced around each other to ease the jar of Dad's thin limbs taking one step after the other as he endured the suffering. Any inquiry about his condition always received the same response—a fervent "Good." It was soon evident that he was reporting on the condition of his spirit and not his physical body.

As we walked toward the bridge the sun reached through the clouds, casting shadows on the lake in the distance. The reflection of the mountains repeated itself in the water; and the feathery clouds, tinted a delicate pink, gave a glow to the valley before us.

"The world is so beautiful, and it's been a good year," Dad remarked, pausing to get a better look at the lake and the sky.

"But, Dad, how can you possibly say that?" I questioned.

Then in the same tone he had often used to counsel me as a child, he explained: "You can't ever look at one little part alone. You must see the whole picture. Just look at the beauties all around us. It's been a good year."

"Dad," I asked, "how did you learn to always look at things like that?"

As we sat on the little rock wall in front of a neighbor's house for a brief rest, he continued: "Well, I had to learn to not let things bother me. It was I who must determine how I would feel, not the circumstances around me. I haven't been successful in life, not in financial matters. I've watched others who are much more able than I in every way, but I learned I must be happy with the way things are for me." Again he repeated, "It's been a good year, Ardie, and a good life."

On our way back from the bridge that day, while we supported each other going up the hill, Dad recited what I came to know as his favorite poem by Virginia Opal Myers:

I believe that God created me to be happy,
To enjoy the blessings of life
To be useful to my fellow beings
And an honor to my country.
I believe that trials which beset me today

Are but fiery tests by which my character
　　is strengthened, ennobled and made worthy to
　　enjoy the higher things in life which I
　　believe are in store for me.
I believe that I am the architect of my own fate.
Therefore, I will be master of circumstances
　　and surroundings and not their slaves.
I will not yield to discouragements.
I will trample them under my feet
　　and make them serve as
　　stepping stones to success.
I will conquer my obstacles and turn
　　them into opportunities.

Again we stopped for rest at our familiar spot on the rock
wall. After catching his breath, he continued:

My failures of today will but help to guide me on
　　to victory on the morrow.
The morrow will bring new strength, new hope,
　　new opportunities and new beginnings.
I will be ready to face them with a brave heart,
　　a calm mind, and an undaunted spirit.
In all things, I will do my best
　　and leave the rest to the infinite.

With added emphasis, he concluded:

I will not waste my mental energy by useless worry.
I will learn to dominate my restless thoughts
　　and look on the bright side of things.
I will face the world bravely.
I will not be a coward.
I will assert my God-given birthright as a man.
For I am immortal, and nothing can overcome me.

Finishing the last line, he stood and picked up his cane. He smiled as we locked our arms together and continued on home.

Each new day I eagerly went downstairs in the morning to check with Dad to see when we would go for our walk. One day I found his bedroom door ajar. He was there, kneeling by the bed that he had made, in a clean, fresh shirt that he put on each day in anticipation of a possible special visitor. His head was supported in his hand. I waited outside his door for what seemed a very long time and pondered the two-way communication that I knew was taking place.

Later Dad sat at the table in the kitchen, again resting his head in his hands. In front of him was a tiny dish containing a spoonful of baby food—all he could manage. Reverently he expressed thanks for the food and gratitude for the lessons of each day. Then he added a request that the food might strengthen him as needed and that he might endure to the end. For over forty years I had heard a blessing on the food at each meal, but never before had I witnessed the earnest supplication and deep gratitude expressed in what until then had become a somewhat routine experience for me.

I was full of anticipation for our walk that morning. The bridge was now completed and we could walk across it to the other side.

"Dad," I began, as we leaned against the concrete divider separating the walking path from the traffic lane, "it must be hard these days."

"Hard? Yes, hard," he replied. "But I don't want to be a coward and get out before I am supposed to. I want to learn all I should from this experience, and I want to endure well. And," he added, "I'm ready to go."

"Dad," I said, "that's not being a coward. That's evidence of your faith in the future."

With that, he tapped his cane several times against the concrete bridge and announced, "Ardie, I'm full of anticipation as I think about walking through that door on my graduation day!" Then, more serious, he explained, "The

108

worst thing now, even worse than the pain, is the feeling of being so useless." With this, his eyes filled with tears.

Putting my arm around his shoulder, I tried hard to explain. "But Dad, you're teaching me now just as much as you always have throughout your life. Dad, you're helping me to cross the bridge."

Prompted by the encouragement, he began to share what I think he may have discovered while I waited for him just outside his bedroom door that morning.

"It is a fact, Ardie. The body and the spirit are separate. When this process of separation is witnessed firsthand the meaning of eternal life and resurrection take on a new dimension of understanding. It's like discovering a gift you've had in your possession but never unwrapped; and then you begin to open it, and you are more ready to fully appreciate it because you are prepared to use it for the purpose it was intended for."

There were many serious and sacred moments, but Dad kept his sense of humor and helped us keep ours. Late one night after I thought everyone had retired, I noticed a light in his room. After knocking gently, I entered. There he sat in the subdued light at his desk. Anxious to understand, my heart filled with tenderness and I longed to ease any concern he might be feeling as he sat alone in the night.

"Dad," I questioned, "what are you thinking?"

"Well," he said with a little smile, as he slapped both hands on his pant legs that appeared void of any form within, "I was just thinking of all the money we've spent on this venture; and I've decided that if I had it to do over, I'd buy a good team of horses and a chariot and go up like Elijah!" I hugged him, kissed him good night, and left him in the calm security of his own understanding.

August 2: This morning Dad faithfully finished his daily exercises, then showered, and dressed in a white shirt and tie. His grandchildren had come from Canada to visit for a few days, and this day had been set aside for a very special purpose.

We gathered in the living room surrounding the big chair where Dad sat to conserve his strength. One by one his children first and then his grandchildren knelt on the floor in front of his chair. Placing his hands on our heads one at a time, exercising his patriarchal privilege, he pronounced a father's blessing or a grandfather's blessing. We realized how well he knew each of us and marveled at the wisdom of the counsel he was inspired to give.

September 3: At fast and testimony meeting Dad was the first to arise. "I don't know how many more opportunities I'll have," he began. With a voice still strong, he stood well groomed, with dignity and a radiant countenance. He spoke only briefly but bore testimony as he quoted from Mosiah 3:19:

> . . . becometh a saint through the atonement of Christ the Lord, and becometh as a child, submissive, meek, humble, patient, full of love, willing to submit to all things which the Lord seeth fit to inflict upon him, even as a child doth submit to his father.

That afternoon we sat together as a family and he instructed us further. "The other side becomes very real as you approach the infield," he said. "Those people long gone become alive again, and you begin to anticipate the glorious reunion."

October 12: Today we walked again to the bridge. I carried an aluminum lawn chair with us so Dad could rest at shorter intervals.

October 18: This morning we barely made it to the bridge. We didn't cross over it, just stopped near the side and watched the water in the creek below.

October 19: This morning Dad looked so weary. He got up late, showered, shaved, struggled to get down his spoonful of food, then lay down for a rest. When he awakened, he didn't want to try the bridge today—just a short walk in the backyard would do.

We walked together, examined the remaining roses, then sat in the lawn chairs for a while. He told me that while he was napping many people were talking to him. He spoke of his brother Addison who had passed away a couple of years before. Then he interrupted his report, smiled, and said, "I guess what I have to say you don't understand." He took my hand and said, as he did when I was young, "Don't be concerned, my dear, it's going to be all right."

That night I put fresh, clean sheets on Dad's bed and some of the remaining roses on his nightstand. On his way down the hall to retire he stopped, leaned against the wall, and said, "I must try to do my exercises." With great effort he raised his frail, thin arms twice, barely above his waist, and dropped them. "Darn," he said, "I just can't make it."

Friday, October 30, 5:30 A.M.: The light was on in Dad's room, and Mom was there at his bedside. Dad sat on the edge of the bed, but said he was so tired. We didn't walk this day. Dad stayed in bed, sleeping off and on during the day. By midafternoon I had decided to sit with him. It seemed his eyes were open, yet he wasn't seeing me. I took his hand in mine, a hand that had spanked me and blessed me and caressed me throughout my life. "Dad," I whispered. He didn't respond. "If you know I'm here, please squeeze my hand." I wasn't sure if there was a squeeze, but it didn't seem like it. I bent over and put my cheek next to his very bony cheek, with my hand on the other side of his face. I waited just a second, then straightened up. It was as though his gaze returned from a long way across the bridge. He looked at me just a moment, and in his eyes I saw complete peace. Joy, trust, confidence, and anticipation all mingled together in that look. A tear escaped from the corner of his eye. I pressed my cheek to his again. There are things we cannot find words or even sounds to express, but in that moment we spoke spirit to spirit.

Shortly after, while my sister was with him, our father's eternal spirit left his mortal body. The family gathered together. I could see what had taken place, but what I felt was more real than what I saw. Dad was not there in the body, but he was there with us extending his great strength that had sustained us over the years. We knelt by his bed to give thanks. With tears of gratitude binding us together as a family, we knew that, because of what we had experienced but could not explain, we understood and felt that peace of which he had so often spoke.

Standing on the bridge, I watched the water still bubbling over the rocks below in the freshness of the new morning. I lifted my eyes to the beauties surrounding me. This season, as with each spring before, had brought a release to buds and leaves, to grasses and flowers held captive for a time as a protection against the winter storms. The signs of new life could be seen and even measured against last year's growth. The call of a bird and an answering call from the distance in the early morning seemed to open my ears. Looking at the little lavender and white violets that could barely be seen pushing their way through the dried grass and leaves of last season opened my eyes to new understanding. I beheld the beauty, the ecstasy, the reality of life—eternal life. Dad had told me in the fall that I would feel good as I stood on the bridge in the springtime.

As I climbed back up the hill the echoes from my prairie crowded in, and I rejoiced in the full anticipation of yet another growing season.